INTELLECTUAL PROPERTY IN THE DIGITAL ERA

Protection, Copyright, and the Value of Creations
2024 Edition

Diego Rodrigues

INTELLECTUAL PROPERTY IN THE DIGITAL ERA

Protection, Copyright, and the Value of Creations

2024 Edition
Author: Diego Rodrigues

Published by StudioD21.

Important Note

The codes and scripts presented in this book aim to illustrate the concepts discussed in the chapters, serving as practical examples. These examples were developed in custom, controlled environments, and therefore there is no guarantee that they will work fully in all scenarios. It is essential to check the configurations and customizations of the environment where they will be applied to ensure their proper functioning. We thank you for your understanding.

CONTENTS

GREETINGS!

Hello, dear reader!

It is with great enthusiasm that I welcome you, who have decided to explore the universe of **Intellectual Property** (PI) — an essential field for protecting and valuing ideas, creations and innovations in an increasingly globalized and digital world. Your choice to dedicate time and attention to this topic demonstrates not only an interest in strategic knowledge, but also a commitment to the future of your creations and ventures.

Intellectual property is not just a technical area; it is the foundation of innovation, creativity and economic competitiveness. This book has been carefully developed to be the most complete guide possible, covering laws, international standards, case studies, and strategies that serve a global audience, from artists and developers to large companies and startups.

Throughout the chapters, you will be guided by a clear and objective approach, which integrates theory and practice. Whether you want to understand the fundamentals of copyright and patents or navigate the complexities of e-commerce and global infringements, this book is designed to turn knowledge into action, offering tools and insights applicable to your context, regardless of industry or country.

We live in an era where the protection of ideas is as crucial as their conception. Mastering IP concepts and practices means being prepared to face challenges on a global scale and take advantage of the opportunities that arise in a constantly changing market.

More than a simple guide, this book is a strategic companion on your journey to understanding and applying intellectual property effectively. It was structured to fill editorial gaps, meet the demands of professionals, academics and entrepreneurs and become an indispensable reference.

Get ready to delve into deep, practical and up-to-date content that will bring clarity to an often complex but absolutely necessary topic. This is the first step to protecting, valuing and expanding your ideas and creations.

I wish you an excellent read and much success on the path you are about to take!

Let's explore the power and importance of intellectual property? So, let's go!

ABOUT THE AUTHOR

www.linkedin.com/in/diegoexpertai

Best-Seller Author, Diego Rodrigues is an International Consultant and Writer specializing in Market Intelligence, Technology and Innovation. With 42 international certifications from institutions such as IBM, Google, Microsoft, AWS, Cisco, and Boston University, Ec-Council, Palo Alto and META.

Rodrigues is an expert in Artificial Intelligence, Machine Learning, Data Science, Big Data, Blockchain, Connectivity Technologies, Ethical Hacking and Threat Intelligence.

Since 2003, Rodrigues has developed more than 200 projects for important brands in Brazil, USA and Mexico. In 2024, he consolidates himself as one of the largest new generation authors of technical books in the world, with more than 180 titles published in six languages.

BOOK PRESENTATION

Hello, dear reader!

Welcome to this complete guide on **INTELLECTUAL PROPERTY IN THE DIGITAL ERA: Protection, Copyright and Value of Creations**. This book was designed especially for you who, in the midst of a world in constant transformation, recognize the importance of understanding and applying the concepts of intellectual property (IP) effectively. Whether you are a creator, entrepreneur, developer, or legal professional, this book is your ally to confidently navigate the complexities of this crucial topic.

The Importance of Intellectual Property in the Global Scenario

Intellectual property is at the heart of innovation and creativity. It is the driving force behind the development of revolutionary technologies, landmark artistic works, and market-shaping global brands. In a connected economy, where ideas are as valuable as products, understanding how to protect your creations is more than a necessity — it's an essential strategy.

This book addresses intellectual property as a practical and strategic tool. It's not just about protecting what you create, but about understanding how to maximize the value of your ideas, expand their reach, and prevent others from taking unfair advantage of them.

Who This Book Was Made For

This guide is aimed at a broad audience, including:

1. **Writers and Authors** – Professionals who want to protect books, scripts and other textual content.
2. **Entrepreneurs and Startups** – Innovative companies that seek to register brands, protect innovations and

create competitive differences.

3. **Digital Artists and Creators** – Designers, photographers, musicians and other professionals in the creative economy.
4. **Software Developers** – Specialists who create technological solutions and need to protect codes and algorithms.
5. **Academics and Researchers** – Those who produce scientific works and seek technology transfer.
6. **IP Consultants and Managers** – Professionals who deal with contracts, patent portfolios and licensing.
7. **Lawyers and Legal Professionals** – Interested in expanding their technical knowledge in IP.
8. **Small and Self-Employed Businesses** – Who want to understand how to protect their brands and creations.

How This Book Was Structured

Each chapter is designed to offer a balance between theory and practice, ensuring that you have both the necessary background and practical tools to apply the knowledge in your everyday life. Below, I present an overview of the chapters, highlighting what you can expect from each of them:

Chapter 1: Introduction to Intellectual Property

This chapter provides an overview of what intellectual property is, its relevance in the global economy and how it influences markets, from e-commerce to creative industries. It is the starting point for understanding how IP has become an indispensable strategic asset.

Chapter 2: History and Evolution of IP

A journey through the evolution of IP, from the Berne Convention to global treaties such as TRIPS. You will see how regulations have been shaped over time to meet the demands of an ever-changing world.

Chapter 3: Copyright

Here, we explore copyright laws and how they vary between jurisdictions. We include practical examples and real cases, showing how to protect literary, audiovisual and digital works.

Chapter 4: Brands and Business Identity

This chapter is dedicated to trademark registration and protection. You will understand how the Madrid Protocol facilitates international registration and see examples of well-known brands and their global management.

Chapter 5: Patents

We unveil the patent registration process, explaining the patentability criteria and how the Patent Cooperation Treaty (PCT) simplifies the protection of inventions in multiple countries.

Chapter 6: Industrial Design

You'll learn the difference between design and patent, as well as protection strategies and case studies that highlight the importance of industrial design in sectors such as fashion and technology.

Chapter 7: Trade Secrets

This chapter covers protecting strategic and confidential information, offering practical examples and explaining how to implement effective security policies.

Chapter 8: Licensing and International Contracts

Learn how to structure IP contracts that work in a global context, from essential clauses to licensing examples for startups and multinationals.

Chapter 9: IP in Electronic Commerce

Discover how to protect brands and products on global marketplaces, deal with digital piracy and apply strategies to protect your online business.

Chapter 10: Infringements and International Disputes

This chapter explores the main types of infractions and how to resolve them on a global stage. You will learn about alternative dispute resolution methods and see analyzes of iconic cases.

Chapter 11: Technology Transfer

We show how universities and companies can transform innovations into economic assets, with examples of successful technology transfer.

Chapter 12: Artificial Intelligence and IP

The debate about authorship of works generated by artificial intelligence is addressed, in addition to examples of legislation and future challenges.

Chapter 13: Strategic IP Management

Learn how to manage an IP portfolio, value assets and maximize their potential in different markets.

Chapter 14: IP in the Creative Industry

This chapter highlights the importance of IP in sectors such as music, fashion, film and games, with practical examples and global data.

Chapter 15: IP and Health

We explore pharmaceutical patents and ethical questions about access to medicines and innovation in healthcare.

Chapter 16: Sustainability and IP

How IP encourages sustainable innovation and protects green technologies that shape the future of the planet.

Chapter 17: Traditional Knowledge and Biopiracy

This chapter focuses on the protection of traditional knowledge and how global conventions, such as Nagoya, seek to combat biopiracy.

Chapter 18: IP in Startups

Practical strategies for startups to protect their innovations and scale sustainably.

Chapter 19: Education and Research

We address copyright challenges in academic research and strategies for technology transfer in educational institutions.

Chapter 20: Economic Impacts of IP

A dive into data and analysis on how IP drives global economies and strategic sectors.

Chapter 21: Future Legal Challenges

We explore gaps in current legislation and how it can evolve to meet technological demands.

Chapter 22: IP in the Public Sector

The relevance of IP in public policies, with examples of governments that use innovation as a driver of growth.

Chapter 23: Global Tools for PI

A practical analysis of software and platforms that help manage and protect IP globally.

Chapter 24: Ethics and IP

Discussions on the balance between protection of ideas and public access, with relevant ethical reflections.

Chapter 25: Practical Guide

We finish with a step-by-step guide on how to apply IP concepts in your daily life, with ready-made models and checklists.

Why This Book Is Essential

By deciding to read this book, you are investing in knowledge that can transform your ideas and creations into valuable and protected assets. This is a practical guide, updated and adaptable to global demands, making it an indispensable reference.

I wish you a transformative read full of learning. Let's walk this path together? Your intellectual property journey starts now!

CHAPTER 1: INTRODUCTION TO INTELLECTUAL PROPERTY

Intellectual Property (IP) is the set of rights that protect creations of the human intellect. It includes technological innovations, literary and artistic works, brands, industrial designs and other intangible assets that have economic and cultural value. IP covers copyrights, trademarks, patents, trade secrets, and industrial designs, among others. These rights grant creators and innovators control over how their creations are used, encouraging the development of new ideas and technologies.

Intellectual property rights not only protect the interests of creators, but also promote innovation by allowing individuals and companies to recoup investments made in research and development. By protecting ideas, IP helps to establish a balance between the public interest and private encouragement of creativity and innovation, creating an environment conducive to economic and social progress.

The economic importance of IP is rooted in its ability to create intangible assets that generate substantial value for companies and individuals. Patents allow companies to monetize technological innovations, guaranteeing a period of exclusivity in the market. Trademarks help establish a company's identity and reputation, creating consumer loyalty. Copyright protects artistic and literary works, ensuring that creators are appropriately rewarded.

In addition to its economic impact, IP has significant cultural and social implications. Protecting intellectual property preserves cultural heritage by ensuring that traditions, indigenous knowledge and artistic expressions are recognized and protected from misappropriation. IP also plays a crucial role in protecting innovations that contribute to social well-being, such as medical advances, green technologies and solutions to global problems.

To illustrate the scope of IP, consider the development of a new drug. A pharmaceutical company can invest years in research, development and clinical trials to create an effective medicine. Without patent protection, other companies could copy the product and commercialize it, undermining the incentive for initial investment. With the patent, the company holds exclusive production and sales rights for a limited period, guaranteeing a return on investment.

Another example of IP in action is in the technology sector. Software developers often use copyrights to protect code and algorithms, while trademarks identify and promote products in the marketplace. Consider a successful app: the user interface can be protected as industrial design, the logo as a trademark, and the underlying code as copyright. This demonstrates how IP can work in an integrated way, protecting multiple aspects of a single creation.

The cultural impact of IP can be observed in the preservation of traditional knowledge. Indigenous knowledge often faces the risk of biopiracy, where companies exploit natural resources and associated knowledge without consent or compensation. IP protection can ensure that communities are recognized and rewarded for the use of their resources and knowledge, promoting ethical and sustainable business practices.

The role of IP in society also includes ethical and access issues. One of the contemporary debates revolves around the balance between pharmaceutical patent protection and access to medicines in developing countries. While patents encourage innovation, they can also restrict access to vital treatments due to high costs. International organizations and global treaties seek to address these challenges, promoting a balance that benefits both innovators and populations in need.

Global recognition of the importance of IP has led to the creation of international agreements and organizations. The World Intellectual Property Organization (WIPO) promotes the harmonization of IP laws between countries, facilitating the protection of intellectual assets in a globalized economy. Treaties such as the Agreement on Trade-Related Aspects of Intellectual Property Rights (TRIPS) establish minimum standards of protection, ensuring that IP rights are respected in all member countries.

Although IP is widely recognized as essential, its concept is not always simple to understand. An important point to consider is that intellectual property does not protect ideas in themselves, but rather the expression or materialization of these ideas. This means that an idea for a novel cannot be protected, but the written text can. Likewise, a mathematical formula cannot be patented, but its practical application in a technology can be protected.

IP also plays a central role in international trade. Companies operating in global markets face challenges such as piracy and counterfeiting, which can damage their brands and reduce profits. To combat these problems, international organizations and governments have implemented strict policies and advanced technologies, such as blockchain, to monitor and protect IP rights.

The digital era has introduced new challenges and opportunities for IP. Technologies such as artificial intelligence (AI) raise questions about authorship and ownership of machine-generated creations. Furthermore, the ease of reproducing and sharing content on the internet has made it more difficult to protect copyrights and combat piracy. On the other hand, technology also offers innovative tools to manage and protect IP, such as digital tagging systems and online registration platforms.

For example, in software development, it is common for developers to use open source licenses to share and collaborate on projects while protecting their copyrights. Here's a simple example of copyrighted Python code:

python

```python
# Copyright (c) 2024, [Your Name]. All rights reserved.
# Redistribution and use in source and binary forms, with or without
# modification, are permitted provided that the following conditions are met:
# [List conditions here]

def calculate_area(radius):
    """
    Calculate the area of a circle given its radius.
    :param radius: float - radius of the circle
    :return: float - area of the circle
    """
    pi = 3.14159
    return pi * (radius ** 2)

radius = 5
print(f"The area of the circle is: {calculate_area(radius)}")
```

This script, although simple, may be copyrighted. Additionally, terms of use and distribution can be specified through licenses, such as MIT or GPL, which define how the code can be reused and modified by third parties.

As the global economy becomes increasingly dependent on intangible assets, IP will continue to be a fundamental pillar of progress. This book is designed to not only provide theoretical knowledge about IP, but also equip you with the practical tools needed to protect and value your creations. Each concept presented will be explored in detail, with clear examples and practical applications.

By understanding and applying IP principles, you will be strategically positioning yourself in a highly competitive market, where the ability to protect and monetize your creations can be the difference between success and failure. Whether you are an artist, entrepreneur, researcher or legal professional, mastering IP is essential to ensure your ideas are recognized, protected and valued.

CHAPTER 2: HISTORY AND EVOLUTION OF IP

The history of intellectual property (IP) is marked by international events and treaties that shaped the legal and structural bases for the protection of human creations over the centuries. Since the first organized efforts to protect innovations and creative works, IP has evolved to become an essential pillar on the global economic stage, influencing the way ideas, brands and innovations are managed across different markets.

The initial records of intellectual property protection date back to antiquity, when governments granted exclusive privileges to inventors. However, it was during the Renaissance period in Europe that the first organized structures emerged to guarantee copyrights and patents. In 1474, the Republic of Venice enacted one of the first patent laws, establishing that inventors could register their creations and obtain exclusivity for a limited period. This encouraged innovation and prevented indiscriminate copying.

With the advent of the Industrial Revolution in the 18th century, the need for a robust system of intellectual protection became evident. The growth of industry and international trade brought new demands for standardized rules that protected inventors and creators across national borders. It was in this context that the Paris Convention emerged in 1883, a historic milestone in the evolution of IP.

The Paris Convention was the first international industrial property treaty and aimed to ensure that inventors had rights recognized in different member countries. This treaty covered patents, trademarks and industrial designs, establishing fundamental principles such as equal treatment between foreigners and citizens. This agreement also introduced the concept of "priority", allowing inventors time to apply for protection in multiple countries after first registering.

At the same time, the Berne Convention of 1886 was another milestone in the protection of intellectual property, focused on copyright. This international treaty established rules to protect literary and artistic works, ensuring that authors had automatic rights to their creations in member countries. The Berne Convention emphasized that protection did not require registration but applied automatically, recognizing creative work on a global scale.

In the early 20th century, the need for global coordination led to the creation of organizations such as the World Intellectual Property Organization (WIPO), founded in 1967. WIPO played a crucial role in harmonizing IP laws across countries and promoting innovation and creativity. Over time, WIPO began to administer several treaties, strengthening the legal framework for IP at an international level.

The Agreement on Trade-Related Aspects of Intellectual Property Rights (TRIPS), adopted in 1994, was another significant milestone in the evolution of IP. This agreement, administered by the World Trade Organization (WTO), established minimum standards of protection for IP rights in all member countries. It also introduced mechanisms to resolve disputes between nations, ensuring that IP rights were applied uniformly in international trade.

The historical importance of TRIPS can be seen in its impact on emerging markets. Many developing countries faced challenges in implementing the provisions of the agreement, as this required significant changes to their national legislation. However, TRIPS also opened doors to international cooperation, encouraging foreign investment and strengthening global trade.

Throughout the 21st century, IP has continued to evolve,

adapting to the demands of a digital and globalized world. The advancement of technology has brought challenges and opportunities, such as the protection of software, algorithms and digital creations. A contemporary example is discussions about artificial intelligence (AI) and its ability to generate original works. Issues such as authorship and rights over AI creations are still being debated, demonstrating how IP continues to expand and adapt.

In the pharmaceutical sector, IP has played a central role, especially during pandemics and global health crises. Patents on medicines and vaccines often raise debates about the balance between encouraging innovation and ensuring universal access. The COVID-19 pandemic exemplified these challenges, when mechanisms such as the WHO patent pool were introduced to share technology and accelerate the production of treatments.

IP has also had a significant impact on the technology sector. Companies like Apple, Google and Microsoft base much of their competitive advantage on intangible assets, including patents, trademarks and copyrights. These tech giants demonstrate how IP can drive innovation and protect business models in highly competitive markets.

E-commerce is another example of how IP influences markets. With the growth of platforms such as Amazon, Alibaba and eBay, protecting brands and products has become essential to combat counterfeiting and ensure consumer trust. Advanced tools such as blockchain are being used to monitor and protect IP rights, demonstrating the integration between technology and intangible asset management.

From a cultural perspective, IP contributes to the preservation of indigenous traditions and knowledge. Global initiatives, such as the Convention on Biological Diversity, aim to protect traditional knowledge and genetic resources against biopiracy. These efforts ensure that indigenous communities are recognized and rewarded for their contributions, promoting social justice and sustainability.

To highlight the evolution of IP, consider the following patent registration example, which illustrates modern documentation and submission requirements:

text

Title: Innovative Solar Panel Design for Efficient Energy Conversion
Abstract: A new design for solar panels that increases energy conversion efficiency by 25%. This innovation utilizes a multi-layer coating to optimize light absorption and minimize heat loss.
Claims:
1. A solar panel comprising a multi-layer coating for enhanced energy conversion.
2. A method for applying the multi-layer coating to solar panel surfaces.
Description: This invention provides a detailed methodology for manufacturing the proposed solar panels, including diagrams and data supporting its increased efficiency.

This example demonstrates how patents are structured to protect technological innovations, highlighting the importance of a clear and detailed description to ensure legal protection.

The history of IP is a journey of adaptation and innovation, reflecting the needs of different eras. From the earliest legislation in Venice to modern treaties administered by WIPO and WTO, IP has been a central element in economic, cultural and technological progress. With the continued advancement of technology and globalization, IP will continue to play a vital role in promoting creativity and protecting the rights of creators around the world.

CHAPTER 3: COPYRIGHT

Copyright is one of the pillars of intellectual property, protecting literary, artistic, scientific and intellectual works in various forms. This system guarantees the author control over the use and distribution of their creations, allowing them to be fairly rewarded for their work. The global copyright structure reflects an ongoing effort to harmonize standards across different jurisdictions, ensuring the protection and recognition of works on an international scale.

The concept of copyright is based on the idea that creativity should be encouraged, and creators need legal protection to prevent unauthorized uses of their works. These rights generally include moral and patrimonial prerogatives. Moral rights ensure that the author is recognized for his creation and that his work is not altered in a way that is harmful to its integrity. Patrimonial rights allow the author to monetize their creation, granting licenses or selling usage rights.

The Berne Convention, signed in 1886, was a landmark in international copyright protection. It established fundamental principles that are still widely followed. Among them, the principle of automatic protection stands out, whereby a work is protected simply by the fact of its creation, without the need for registration. Another principle is reciprocity, ensuring that signatory countries treat foreign works in the same way they treat national works.

Despite the Berne Convention, significant differences still exist between jurisdictions. In the United States, for example, copyright registration, although not mandatory, offers additional legal benefits, such as the possibility of claiming legal damages in lawsuits. In the European Union, the focus is on a harmonized system, where rights are uniform among member states. In China, efforts have been made to improve copyright protection, but challenges such as piracy and legal enforcement persist.

The digital environment presents unique challenges for copyright. The ease of reproduction and dissemination of content over the internet requires new approaches to protect creators. Platforms like YouTube and Spotify use content identification algorithms to monitor the use of protected works and ensure that rights holders receive compensation. However, these solutions are not always perfect, especially when it comes to derivative works or fair use.

The issue of fair use is particularly important in jurisdictions such as the United States, where the doctrine allows parts of a work to be used without permission in contexts such as criticism, parody, or academic research. This concept, however, is not uniformly applied throughout the world, creating barriers to the transnational use of works. For example, a video created in the United States that uses portions of a song under the fair use doctrine may face restrictions in countries with stricter legislation.

To illustrate how copyright works in practice, consider an author who wants to protect a book and publish it across multiple digital platforms. After creation, the author may choose to register the work with a copyright office, such as the United States Copyright Office. This registration not only provides proof of authorship, but also facilitates protection against unauthorized copying. With the book published on digital platforms, the author can monitor its dissemination using monitoring tools based on digital watermarking technology.

In the case of music, many artists use services like YouTube's Content ID to identify and manage the use of their works. The system analyzes the content uploaded to the platform and compares it with a database of protected works. If a match is found, the rights holder can choose to monetize the video, block it, or simply monitor usage. This type of technology reflects efforts to modernize copyright protection in a digital environment.

Software and application development is also closely linked to copyright. Source codes are protected like literary works, ensuring that developers maintain control over their creation. Here's an example of simple copyrighted code:

python

```python
# Copyright (c) 2024, [Your Name]. All rights reserved.
# This code may not be reproduced or distributed without permission.

def encrypt_message(message, key):
    """
    Encrypts a message using a simple substitution cipher.
    :param message: str - The message to encrypt
    :param key: int - The shift value for the cipher
    :return: str - The encrypted message
    """
    encrypted = ''.join(
        chr((word(char) - 65 + key) % 26 + 65) if char.isupper() else
        chr((ord(char) - 97 + key) % 26 + 97) if char.islower() else char
        for char in message
    )
    return encrypted

original_message = "HelloWorld"
encryption_key = 3
print(f"Encrypted Message: {encrypt_message(original_message, encryption_key)}")
```

This simple encryption script can be used as an example of how copyright protects intellectual creations in the field of programming. It ensures that the author maintains control over the use and distribution of the code.

Although copyright is a powerful system, it is not perfect. Piracy remains a global challenge, especially in countries where copyright law enforcement is weak. Furthermore, the integration of artificial intelligence into creative processes raises questions about the ownership of machine-generated works. For example, who owns the rights to a song composed entirely by AI? These challenges require innovative solutions and ongoing legislative debates.

Copyright protection is essential to encourage creativity and innovation, but it is also necessary to strike a balance that allows fair use and access to works. In an increasingly interconnected world, international cooperation is vital to address challenges and create a copyright system that benefits both creators and consumers. The continuous evolution of technologies and the improvement of legislation promise to shape the future of this fundamental area of intellectual property.

CHAPTER 4: BRANDS AND BUSINESS IDENTITY

Brands and commercial identity play a fundamental role in building businesses and differentiating products and services in the global market. A brand is more than a visual symbol; it encapsulates a company's reputation, quality, and promise to its consumers. Protecting brands is a priority for companies seeking to grow in competitive markets, as the brand is a high-value intangible asset that can directly impact consumer trust and loyalty.

Trademark registration is one of the most effective methods of protecting business identity. This process gives owners the exclusive right to use and the ability to take legal action against unauthorized uses. In a globalized scenario, the Madrid Protocol, administered by the World Intellectual Property Organization (WIPO), simplifies international trademark registration, allowing companies to protect their commercial identity in several countries with a single application.

The Madrid Protocol significantly reduces the complexity of registering trademarks in multiple jurisdictions. It operates with a centralized system, where applicants can register a trademark in more than 130 participating countries through a single form, using a common language and paying a single fee. This approach saves time and resources, making brand protection more accessible for businesses of all sizes.

To better understand how the Madrid Protocol works, consider the case of a technology startup that wants to expand its business to the international market. After creating a unique visual identity and registering the brand in its country of origin, the company decides to register the same brand in several international markets. Using the Madrid Protocol, the process can be initiated by submitting a single request to WIPO, specifying target countries. If the brand is approved in these countries, the company will have exclusive rights in all of them, protecting its commercial identity globally.

The importance of trademark protection can be illustrated through practical cases. A large fashion multinational faced a significant case of trademark infringement in emerging markets. Local companies were using a similar logo to market low-quality products, confusing consumers and damaging the original brand's reputation. The multinational used its trademark rights to sue infringing companies, ensuring the protection of its identity and the integrity of its products.

Trademark infringements are frequent challenges, especially in markets where enforcement is weak. Counterfeit products, also known as counterfeits, are one of the most common forms of trademark infringement. Not only do they harm legitimate businesses, they can also put consumers at risk, especially in industries like food, medicine and electronics. Tools like blockchain are being used to combat counterfeiting by providing a secure way to track the authenticity of products.

In the digital sector, brands face unique challenges. Internet domains, for example, can be registered by third parties to exploit the recognition of an existing brand, a practice known as cybersquatting. Companies facing this issue can use the Uniform Domain Name Dispute Resolution Policy (UDRP), created by WIPO, to recover domains efficiently.

The process of registering a trademark involves several steps, from initial research to ensure there are no conflicting marks to submitting the application and following up on possible objections. Here is an example of a structured trademark application:

Trademark Registration Request:

- **Brand Name:** TechNova
- **Logo:** A stylized star with the name "TechNova" in a futuristic font.
- **Description of Products/Services:** Software development and technology services.
- **Target Countries:** United States, Canada, Germany, Japan.
- **Nice classification:** Class 42 (Information Technology Services).
- **Proof of Use:** Product catalogue, official website, advertising campaigns.
- **Declaration:** The "TechNova" brand does not infringe the rights of third parties.

This request would be submitted to the responsible body in the country of origin or directly through the Madrid Protocol, depending on the international expansion strategy.

Brand protection also includes ongoing management of its use. Companies must monitor the market to identify possible violations, such as imitations or misuse of logos and slogans. Furthermore, renewing registrations within the stipulated deadlines is crucial to maintaining exclusivity rights.

Brand protection cases often highlight the importance of a robust strategy. A company in the food sector, for example, decided to expand into Asia without previously registering its brand in that market. A local company took the opportunity to register the brand in its name, forcing the multinational to face a long legal process to recover its rights. This case highlights the importance of anticipating trademark protection in target markets.

In addition to registration, internal awareness is also essential to prevent accidental breaches. Marketing and design departments must be trained to create visual identities that do not infringe on third-party rights. Trademark search tools, available in global databases, can help with this process.

Commercial identity is a strategic asset that goes beyond logos and names. Elements such as packaging, slogans, color palettes and even distinctive sounds can be registered and protected. In some cases, product shapes or store layouts also receive protection, as in the case of Apple store design, which is protected as a trademark.

To effectively manage brands, many companies use intellectual property portfolio management software. These systems allow brand owners to monitor their registrations, track renewals, and identify potential conflicts. Additionally, digital monitoring tools analyze online brand usage, identifying violations in real time.

The evolution of trademark legislation reflects the need to adapt to new realities. On the global stage, treaties such as the Madrid Protocol and the Paris Convention remain vital tools, but digital challenges require legislative and technological innovations. Solutions such as artificial intelligence are being explored to help with the registration process and conflict analysis, making the system more agile and efficient.

Protecting brands and business identity is an ongoing responsibility that requires strategic planning and swift action against violations. Companies that invest in protecting their brands not only protect their assets, but also strengthen their market presence and build long-term relationships with their consumers. With the support of international structures and the use of advanced technologies, brands can thrive in an increasingly competitive global environment.

CHAPTER 5: PATENTS

Patents are one of the central elements of intellectual property, protecting inventions and granting inventors exclusive rights to exploit their creations for a limited period of time. They encourage innovation by providing a financial return for those who invest in research and development. To obtain global or multi-jurisdictional protection, the patent registration system is fundamental, with the Patent Cooperation Treaty (PCT) being a valuable resource in this process.

The PCT is administered by the World Intellectual Property Organization (WIPO) and simplifies patent registration in several countries. Instead of filing separate applications in each jurisdiction, the PCT allows inventors to submit a single international application. This system does not grant patents directly, but it facilitates the registration process in more than 150 member countries, saving time and resources.

The PCT registration process begins with the submission of an international application to WIPO or the competent national or regional patent office. This application must include a clear and detailed description of the invention, claims defining the scope of protection, technical drawings (if applicable) and a summary. After filing, the application undergoes an international search conducted by a designated authority, which provides a preliminary report indicating the novelty, inventive step and industrial applicability of the invention.

After the search stage, the inventor has an additional period to decide in which countries they wish to seek protection, generally up to 30 months from the priority date. This time window allows inventors to evaluate the commercial potential of their inventions in different markets before incurring local registration costs.

For example, a biotechnology company develops a new method for synthesizing proteins. Using the PCT system, she can register her invention and obtain a preliminary technical feasibility report. Based on this report, the company decides to prioritize markets where the method is most profitable, such as the United States, European Union, Japan and China. After identifying the markets, it continues with the national registration phase in these countries.

Patents follow specific criteria that vary slightly between jurisdictions, although most share basic principles. These criteria include novelty, inventive (or non-obvious) step and industrial applicability. Despite the similarities, there are notable differences in the analysis and registration process between large markets, such as the United States, European Union, Japan and China.

In the United States, the patent system is administered by the United States Patent and Trademark Office (USPTO). A hallmark feature is the "first-to-invent" principle, which was replaced by "first-to-invent" following the American Inventions Act (AIA) of 2011. This means that priority is given to the first filing, rather than the first creator, aligning the system with international practices. Another peculiarity is the widespread use of provisional patents, which allow inventors to obtain an initial priority date without the need to file a full application immediately.

In the European Union, the European Patent Office (EPO) oversees the registration process, allowing inventors to seek protection in multiple member countries through a single application. The approval of the unitary patent package in 2023 brought more uniformity, allowing automatic protection in all participating countries. However, each country retains the right to litigate independently, which can create legal complexities.

Japan operates under a highly strict patent system administered by the Japan Patent Office (JPO). Speed of processing is a distinguishing feature, with Japan often issuing decisions on patent applications more quickly than other jurisdictions.

However, the analysis is extremely detailed, reflecting the country's emphasis on quality and technical innovation.

China has emerged as one of the largest markets for patent registration, leading in annual application volume. The China National Intellectual Property Administration (CNIPA) administers the system, which has evolved significantly in recent decades. Although the process is efficient and initial costs are lower than in many Western countries, enforcement of patent rights remains a challenge in less regulated markets.

The importance of aligning patent registration with local peculiarities is evident. A company seeking protection in the United States may opt for a provisional application to save time, while in Europe it may prefer to use the unitary patent system to save on maintenance fees. In Japan, focusing on the technical clarity of the invention will be essential for approval, while in China it is important to ensure that the application is detailed enough to avoid disputes.

In addition to legal criteria, the wording of the patent application is a critical aspect. Claims define the scope of protection and must be written precisely to avoid ambiguity. Here is a simplified patent claim example:

text

Title: Advanced Energy Storage System
Abstract: A system for storing energy with enhanced efficiency using graphene-based supercapacitors.
Claims:
1. A supercapacitor comprising graphene electrodes with a specific surface area exceeding 2000 m^2/g, enhancing charge storage capacity.
2. A method for manufacturing the supercapacitor described in Claim 1, involving chemical vapor deposition of graphene layers.
3. A system integrating the supercapacitor with solar energy panels for improved energy storage and release.

Description: The invention relates to the development of high-performance energy storage systems leveraging the unique properties of graphene, offering significant improvements in capacity and durability.

This example highlights how the claims must be clear, detailed and focused on innovative aspects, while the description provides the technical context necessary to understand the invention.

Patent management does not end with registration. Companies must regularly monitor the market to identify possible infringements and maintain rights by paying maintenance fees. Enforcement may also involve litigation to protect the rights of the holder in the event of unauthorized use.

Patents play a critical role in technology, healthcare and energy industries, where innovation is the key competitive differentiator. Technology companies often accumulate patent portfolios to protect inventions and create barriers to entry. In the pharmaceutical sector, patents guarantee exclusivity in medicines, allowing a return on investments in research. However, this also raises ethical debates, especially regarding access to medicines in developing countries.

The digital era has brought new challenges to the patent system. Emerging technologies such as artificial intelligence raise questions about whether AI-generated inventions can be patented. Furthermore, the convergence of technologies means that inventions can fall into multiple categories, requiring innovative approaches to application writing and analysis.

Patent registration through the PCT is an essential tool for inventors seeking global protection. However, it is crucial to understand regional differences and plan strategically to maximize business impact and legal protection. As technologies and markets continue to evolve, the role of patents remains vital in promoting innovation and strengthening the global economy.

CHAPTER 6: INDUSTRIAL DESIGN

Industrial design plays a fundamental role in differentiating products and creating added value in the global market. It is responsible for the shape and appearance of a product, as well as characteristics such as colors, textures and visual elements that make it unique and attractive to consumers. Legal protection of industrial design is essential to prevent unauthorized copying and ensure that companies and creators can monetize their creative efforts.

Global protection for industrial design is governed by a combination of international treaties and national legislation. Among the main international instruments is the Hague Agreement, administered by the World Intellectual Property Organization (WIPO). This system allows creators to register their designs in multiple countries through a single application, saving time and resources.

A legally protected industrial design grants the holder the exclusive right to use it, license its application and prevent third parties from using it without authorization. Unlike other forms of intellectual property, such as patents or trademarks, industrial design is focused exclusively on the aesthetic aspects of a product, from household appliances to vehicles and electronic devices.

The process of registering an industrial design begins with clearly defining the design to be protected. This includes presenting detailed images or graphic representations that show the product from different angles. The design description should be objective, focusing on the visual elements that differentiate the product.

Industrial design legislation varies between jurisdictions. In the European Union, for example, the Registered Community Design

(RCD) system offers uniform protection across all member countries, simplifying the process for companies operating in the European market. In the United States, design is protected through design patents, which have a more technical process but offer a high level of protection. In Japan, the system is known for its efficiency, requiring detailed descriptions and accurate representations of the design.

China, as one of the largest markets in the world, has particularities. The Chinese industrial design system has advanced significantly in recent years, but still faces challenges related to oversight and piracy. Efficient protection requires companies to adopt proactive strategies such as early registration and market surveillance.

Case studies highlight the importance of industrial design in commercial strategy. A global technology company launched a smartphone with an innovative design that included curved edges and seamless integration between hardware and software. By registering industrial design in key markets, the company guaranteed exclusivity, preventing competitors from copying its appearance. This registration allowed the company to not only consolidate its market position, but also increase the perceived value of its brand.

Another relevant case involves the fashion sector, where shoe, bag and clothing designs often face copying risks. A luxury brand has trademarked the unique design of an iconic bag, which included a unique pattern and distinctive structural details. By identifying counterfeit products at trade shows, the company used its industrial design rights to remove infringing items from the market and reinforce its reputation as a leader in originality.

In product development, digital tools play an increasing role in creating and recording designs. 3D modeling software allows designers to create detailed representations of their concepts, which can be directly used in the registration process. Furthermore, digital platforms enable continuous monitoring of the use of designs registered in global markets, facilitating the identification of infringements.

Below is an example of how an industrial design can be described and documented in a registration application:

Industrial Design Registration Application

- **Design Title:** Modern Office Chair
- **Design Description:** Ergonomic chair with curved back in translucent mesh, padded seat with rounded edges and aluminum base with five wheels. Matte black finish and chrome details.
- **Graphic Representations:** Images from different angles, including front, side, top and back views.
- **Declaration of Originality:** This design is exclusive and was not released to the public before the registration date.
- **Intended Use:** Office and commercial furniture.

This application would be submitted to the competent body, such as the European Union Intellectual Property Office (EUIPO) or the United States Patent and Trademark Office (USPTO), depending on the target market.

Managing industrial design portfolios is essential for companies operating globally. A well-managed portfolio ensures that designs are protected in the relevant markets and that renewals are carried out within legal deadlines. Companies often use specialized software to track their records and identify potential conflicts.

In the digital market, design protection extends to user interfaces (UI) and user experiences (UX). Apps and websites often feature unique layouts and visual elements that can be trademarked as industrial designs. Protecting these elements is crucial for companies that depend on intuitive and attractive interfaces as a competitive differentiator.

In addition to protection, monetizing industrial designs can be a profitable strategy. Companies often license their designs to other organizations, generating additional revenue. This is common in industries like fashion, where big-name brands allow other manufacturers to use their designs in exchange for royalties.

Enforcement against violations of industrial designs is a critical aspect. Companies must actively monitor the market to identify products that infringe their rights. In cases where infractions are detected, legal actions can be taken, from extrajudicial notifications to legal proceedings. Collaborating with specialized lawyers and using technology, such as blockchain, to track the origin of products are effective strategies.

Industrial designs not only protect the aesthetics of products, but also play a strategic role in brand building and market differentiation. The ability to protect, manage and monetize designs is an essential skill for companies in competitive industries. With the right tools and strategies, industrial designs can become valuable assets that drive innovation and global growth.

CHAPTER 7: TRADE SECRETS

Trade secrets represent a special category of intellectual property that protects confidential information of commercial value. They include formulas, methods, processes, techniques, business strategies and other knowledge that give a company a competitive advantage. Unlike patents and trademarks, trade secrets do not require official registration, but depend on protection measures to maintain their confidentiality and legal applicability.

Protecting trade secrets is crucial across industries, from technology and manufacturing to food and financial services. For information to be classified as a commercial secret, it must meet three fundamental criteria: it has economic value because it is secret, it is not publicly known or easily accessible, and it is subject to reasonable protection measures by its holder.

The legal framework for protecting trade secrets varies globally, but treaties such as the TRIPS Agreement provide a common basis. TRIPS requires member countries of the World Trade Organization (WTO) to implement legal protections for confidential information that meet established criteria. In the United States, protection is governed by the Defense of Trade Secrets Act (DTSA), which provides mechanisms for civil prosecution in cases of misappropriation. In the European Union, the Trade Secrets Directive harmonized the laws of Member States, creating a common standard for legal protection and compliance.

A practical example of a trade secret is the Coca-Cola formula, which has been kept strictly confidential for more than a century. Instead of patenting the formula, the company chose to protect it as a trade secret, as registering a patent would require public disclosure of the composition, allowing competitors to replicate it after the patent expires.

Tools to protect trade secrets in multinational companies are essential to ensure confidential information is preserved in diverse and geographically dispersed work environments. A robust strategy starts with implementing clear internal policies that define what information is classified as trade secrets and how it should be treated.

Signing non-disclosure agreements (NDAs) is standard practice for protecting trade secrets. These contracts legally bind employees, suppliers, business partners and other individuals or entities not to disclose confidential information without authorization. Below is an example of an NDA clause that can be used by companies:

text

Confidentiality Agreement Clause:
The receiving party agrees to maintain the confidentiality of all disclosed proprietary information, including but not limited to trade secrets, technical data, customer lists, and financial details. The receiving party shall not disclose, reproduce, or use the proprietary information for any purpose other than the fulfillment of its obligations under this agreement. The obligations under this clause shall survive the termination of this agreement for a period of five (5) years.

In addition to confidentiality agreements, segregation of information is a best practice. This involves limiting access to confidential information to only those employees or departments that truly need it to perform their functions. This approach can be reinforced with the use of access control systems, multi-factor authentication and audit logging to monitor who has accessed certain data.

Multinational companies often face the challenge of protecting trade secrets in jurisdictions with varying levels of legal compliance. In countries where law enforcement is less robust, internal protective measures become even more critical. Investing in regular training for employees about the company's confidentiality policies helps create a culture of protecting information.

Technology plays a central role in protecting trade secrets. Information management systems, such as blockchain-based platforms, can be used to record and monitor access to sensitive data. Blockchain offers an immutable record of transactions, ensuring transparency and traceability. A practical example is the use of smart contracts to automate compliance with NDAs, recording when parties signed the agreement and monitoring subsequent interactions.

Another effective tool is the implementation of data loss prevention (DLP) systems. These systems detect and prevent the unauthorized transfer of confidential information via emails, USB devices or other channels. For example, by configuring DLP policies in an organization, you can block the sending of files containing keywords or identifiers related to trade secrets.

Below, a simple Python script illustrates how a company can implement a basic check for files containing sensitive terms before allowing them to be transferred:

python

```python
def check_confidential_terms(file_path, terms):
    """
    Check if a file contains confidential terms.
    :param file_path: str - Path to the file
    :param terms: list - List of confidential terms to check
    :return: bool - True if terms are found, False otherwise
    """
    try:
        with open(file_path, 'r') as file:
            content = file.read()
            for term in terms:
```

```
            if term in content:
                return True
        return False
    except FileNotFoundError:
        print("File not found.")
        return False

confidential_terms = ["TradeSecret", "Confidential", "Proprietary"]
file_to_check = "document.txt"

if check_confidential_terms(file_to_check, confidential_terms):
    print("Confidential terms detected. Transfer denied.")
else:
    print("No confidential terms found. Transfer allowed.")
```

This script demonstrates a basic approach to identifying and blocking the transfer of files containing sensitive information. In a corporate environment, this functionality can be expanded with integrations into more advanced DLP systems.

Challenges related to protecting trade secrets include not only protecting against internal or external theft, but also mitigating risks associated with collaborating with third parties. Collaborative projects, such as product co-development or service outsourcing, require companies to establish rigorous safeguards to prevent information leaks.

Misappropriation of trade secrets can cause significant financial and reputational harm. Lawsuits are a common avenue for dealing with violations, but they can be time-consuming and expensive. Therefore, prevention is always more effective than cure. Multinational companies must adopt a proactive approach, combining internal policies, advanced technologies and regular training.

Trade secrets remain a powerful tool for protecting a company's unique knowledge and strategies. In a global, digital environment, protection practices need to constantly evolve to keep up with emerging threats. With a combination of legal, technological and cultural measures, it is possible to ensure that trade secrets remain a valuable asset for innovation and competitiveness.

CHAPTER 8: LICENSING AND INTERNATIONAL CONTRACTS

Licensing and international contracts play an essential role in intellectual property, allowing rights holders to monetize their creations and expand their presence in global markets. They ensure that the use of patents, trademarks, copyrights and other assets is regulated, offering protection for both licensors and licensees. For these contracts to be effective, they need to be structured clearly and adapted to multilingual and multicultural contexts.

Structuring multilingual contracts is a common challenge for companies operating globally. Contracts of this type must be written in languages that are understood by all parties involved, ensuring accuracy and eliminating ambiguities. It is common for international contracts to be written in one main language, such as English, with translations into other relevant languages. In these situations, it is essential to include a linguistic predominance clause, specifying which version of the contract will prevail in the event of conflicts of interpretation.

An example of a language predominance clause that can be used in multilingual contracts:

text

Language Clause:
This Agreement is executed in English and [secondary language]. In the event of any conflict or discrepancy between the versions, the English version shall prevail.

In addition to dealing with language barriers, international contracts must consider cultural and legal differences. Jurisdictions can vary significantly in their interpretations of contractual terms, validity standards and enforcement mechanisms. It is crucial that contracts include clauses that define the applicable jurisdiction and forum, as well as the laws that govern the agreement.

An effective licensing agreement typically includes detailed sections that specify the rights granted, the parties' obligations, the duration of the agreement, license fees, and dispute resolution mechanisms. In the international context, contracts often involve additional complexities, such as cross-border taxation and export regulations.

A basic structure for a licensing agreement can be represented as follows:

Structure of an International Licensing Agreement:

1. **Parties to the Contract**: Identification of the licensor (right holder) and licensee (authorized user).
2. **Object of the Contract**: Clear description of the intellectual property rights being licensed, such as a specific patent, trademark, or software.
3. **Territory**: Geographical limitation of the use of licensed rights.
4. **Duration**: Period during which the contract will be in force.
5. **Compensation**: Details of license fees, royalties or other payments.
6. **Obligations of the Parties**: Duties and responsibilities of both parties, such as maintaining confidentiality and complying with local laws.
7. **Use Restrictions**: Specifications about how the licensed rights may or may not be used.
8. **Termination**: Conditions under which the contract can be terminated.
9. **Applicable Law and Dispute Resolution**: Choice of law

governing the contract and mechanisms for handling disputes, such as arbitration or mediation.

10. **Language and Translations**: Declaration on the official language of the contract and validity of translations.

Case studies help illustrate successful licensing and international contract negotiations. One example is the partnership between a North American technology company and an Asian manufacturer to license automotive sensor technology. The contract included territorial exclusivity clauses, allowing the manufacturer to exploit rights in Asia while the licensing company maintained control in other regions. The inclusion of a performance-based royalty clause incentivized the manufacturer to maximize sales, benefiting both parties.

Another example involves licensing a European fashion brand to a partner in the Middle East. The agreement defined detailed quality standards to ensure that products sold under the brand meet the expectations of global consumers. Additionally, it included clauses on the use of digital marketing, specifying that all advertising campaigns must be approved by the licensor to maintain brand consistency.

In the software industry, licensing agreements are critical to protecting the rights of developers while enabling the use of their solutions by global companies. A typical example is the use of enterprise software licenses. Here is an excerpt from a contract that can be used to license software:

text

Software License Agreement:
1. License Grant: The Licensor hereby grants the Licensee a non-exclusive, non-transferable license to use the Software within the agreed territory for internal business purposes only.
2. Fees: The Licensee agrees to pay an annual licensing fee of [amount] and additional fees for updates or support as specified in Schedule A.

3. Restrictions: The Licensee shall not reverse engineer, decompile, or disassemble the Software without prior written consent from the Licensor.

4. Termination: The Licensor may terminate this Agreement if the Licensee breaches any term herein, with a written notice of thirty (30) days.

5. Governing Law: This Agreement shall be governed by the laws of [jurisdiction].

This agreement details the terms of use and applicable restrictions, protecting the licensor's interests while providing clarity to the licensee.

Technology plays an increasing role in the management of international contracts. Digital tools, such as contract management software, help companies monitor due dates, payments, and compliance with terms. Additionally, emerging technologies like blockchain are being explored to record and verify contracts, providing an additional layer of transparency and security.

Another important consideration in international contracts is the impact of local and transnational regulations. For example, in the biotechnology sector, licensing agreements often need to address export and import requirements for genetic materials, ensuring compliance with international conventions such as the Nagoya Protocol.

Dispute resolution mechanisms in international contracts must be carefully chosen to avoid legal complications. Arbitration is often preferred as it offers greater flexibility and neutrality than national courts. Institutions such as the International Chamber of Commerce (ICC) offer widely recognized and respected arbitration services.

Licensing and international contracts are powerful tools for global expansion, but they require meticulous attention to detail and an understanding of legal and cultural complexities. With a well-structured approach and the use of modern technologies, companies can maximize the benefits of their intellectual property rights while minimizing the risks associated with cross-border operations.

CHAPTER 9: IP IN ELECTRONIC COMMERCE

Intellectual property in e-commerce plays a vital role in a digital world where transactions occur quickly and on a global scale. With the proliferation of marketplaces such as Amazon, Alibaba, eBay and social media platforms, the protection of digital assets has become a priority for companies that want to guarantee the authenticity of their products, protect brands and combat illicit practices such as digital piracy and counterfeiting.

In the digital environment, intellectual property assets include trademarks, copyrights, industrial designs and patents. These assets ensure that products and content are recognized as original and protected against misuse. Effective enforcement of intellectual property on marketplaces depends on a combination of advanced technologies, robust policies, and collaboration between platforms and rights owners.

Protecting digital assets on global marketplaces starts with registering trademarks and copyrights in the relevant jurisdictions. Registration ensures that rights holders can take legal action against infringers and request the removal of products or content that violate their rights. Platforms like Amazon and Alibaba offer brand protection programs, which allow rights owners to monitor listings and report infringement directly.

One of the most effective mechanisms for protecting brands is the use of digital monitoring tools that continuously analyze marketplaces for products that use protected trademarks or logos. These tools, often powered by artificial intelligence, identify potentially infringing listings and notify rights owners. Below is an example of a basic Python script that can be used as part of an internal system to identify potential violations in product descriptions:

python

```python
import requests

def check_infringement(keywords, url):
    """
    Check for infringement keywords in a marketplace listing.
    :param keywords: list - List of brand-related keywords to check
    :param url: str - URL of the marketplace listing
    :return: bool - True if infringement keywords are found, False otherwise
    """
    try:
        response = requests.get(url)
        if response.status_code == 200:
            content = response.text.lower()
            for keyword in keywords:
                if keyword.lower() in content:
                    return True
        return False
    except requests.exceptions.RequestException as e:
        print(f"Error fetching URL: {e}")
        return False

keywords_to_check = ["authenticBrand", "officialLogo",
"premiumDesign"]
listing_url = "https://example.com/product-listing"

if check_infringement(keywords_to_check, listing_url):
    print("Potential infringement detected. Take action.")
else:
    print("No infringement detected.")
```

This basic script checks for brand-related keywords in a marketplace listing, alerting administrators to potential violations. In a corporate environment, this approach would be integrated into more complex systems that automatically track thousands of listings.

In addition to technological tools, collaboration between companies and marketplaces is essential to combat digital piracy. Programs like **Amazon Brand Registry** and the **Alibaba Anti-Counterfeiting Alliance** help companies register their brands directly on platforms, making it easier to identify and remove counterfeit products. These programs offer features such as brand authentication, pattern detection, and simplified reporting mechanisms.

However, digital piracy goes beyond counterfeiting products. It also includes the unauthorized distribution of copyrighted content, such as books, films, music and software. File-sharing platforms, social networks and illegal streaming sites are the main channels for this type of activity. To deal with these threats, technologies such as digital watermarking and digital rights management (DRM) systems are widely used.

Digital watermarks are invisible insertions in media files that identify the source and owner of the content. When an unauthorized copy is found, the watermark can be used to track the source of the leak. DRM systems, in turn, control how digital content is accessed, preventing unauthorized copying and restricting use to specific devices.

Below is an example of Python code to add a simple watermark to images, which can be used to protect digital designs:

python

```
from PIL import Image, ImageDraw, ImageFont

def add_watermark(input_image_path, output_image_path,
```

```
watermark_text):
    """

    Add a watermark to an image.
    :param input_image_path: str - Path to the input image
    :param output_image_path: str - Path to save the watermarked
image
    :param watermark_text: str - Text to use as the watermark
    """

    image = Image.open(input_image_path).convert("RGBA")
    watermark = Image.new("RGBA", image.size, (255, 255, 255,
0))
    draw = ImageDraw.Draw(watermark)
    font = ImageFont.load_default()
    text_width, text_height = draw.textsize(watermark_text, font)

    position = (image.size[0] - text_width - 10, image.size[1] -
text_height - 10)
    draw.text(position, watermark_text, fill=(255, 255, 255, 128),
font=font)

    watermarked_image = Image.alpha_composite(image,
watermark)
    watermarked_image.save(output_image_path, "PNG")

input_path = "original_image.png"
output_path = "watermarked_image.png"
watermark = "Protected by BrandName"

add_watermark(input_path, output_path, watermark)
```

The script inserts a watermark into digital images, protecting designs or visual content from unauthorized copying. These methods are useful for designers and photographers who want to protect their creations in the digital environment.

Strategies against digital piracy also include implementing robust compliance policies. Companies must educate their employees, partners and consumers about the risks of piracy and the benefits of supporting legitimate products and content. Additionally, collaboration with governments and international organizations can help strengthen the enforcement of intellectual property laws in different jurisdictions.

Practical cases demonstrate the effectiveness of combined strategies. A large software company was facing widespread piracy of its products on online marketplaces. By implementing a combination of DRM, digital monitoring and direct collaboration with marketplaces, the company was able to significantly reduce the distribution of unauthorized versions of its software. Additionally, targeted educational campaigns have helped increase consumer awareness of the risks associated with using pirated software.

Another example is the fashion sector, where luxury brands face challenges with counterfeit products. Some of these brands use blockchain technology to authenticate their products. By scanning a QR code on a product, consumers can verify its authenticity, trace its origin, and confirm that it was legally produced and distributed.

Intellectual property in e-commerce requires a multifaceted approach that combines technology, collaboration and awareness. Protecting digital assets and combating digital piracy is not just a matter of legal compliance, but also of preserving consumer trust and promoting a fair and innovative market. Companies that invest in proactive strategies are better positioned to thrive in an ever-evolving digital environment.

CHAPTER 10: INFRINGEMENTS AND INTERNATIONAL DISPUTES

Intellectual property infringements are frequent challenges in global markets, where the dissemination of information, products and technologies occurs on an unprecedented scale. These infringements range from copyright violations and trademark counterfeiting to the misuse of patents and industrial designs. When international disputes arise, litigation may be inevitable, but alternative dispute resolution methods have gained prominence as efficient ways of dealing with these issues.

International intellectual property disputes often involve multiple jurisdictions, complicating law enforcement and case resolution. A notable example is the litigation between Apple and Samsung, which has played out in various courts around the world over allegations of patent and industrial design infringement. The dispute began with Apple claiming that Samsung copied the design and features of its products. Decisions varied by jurisdiction, with some courts favoring Apple and others favoring Samsung, demonstrating the legal complexities in cross-border cases.

Another significant case involved the pharmaceutical company Novartis in India. The company sought to protect its drug formula through a patent, but the Indian Supreme Court denied the request, arguing that the formula did not present enough innovation to justify protection. This decision highlighted the strict interpretation of patentability criteria in some jurisdictions, especially in cases related to essential medicines.

These examples illustrate how intellectual property disputes can vary widely depending on local laws, public policies, and economic priorities in each country. For companies operating globally, anticipating these differences and planning appropriate strategies is crucial.

Alternative dispute resolution methods (ADRs) offer effective solutions for dealing with intellectual property infringements without resorting to lengthy and expensive court proceedings. Among the most common methods are arbitration, mediation and direct negotiation.

Arbitration It is often preferred in international disputes due to its confidential nature and the ability for parties to choose intellectual property experts as arbitrators. Arbitration is binding and decisions are generally recognized in various jurisdictions under the 1958 New York Convention. An example of an arbitration clause in an intellectual property contract is shown below:

text

Arbitration Clause:
Any dispute, controversy, or claim arising out of or relating to this Agreement, including the validity, interpretation, or infringement of intellectual property rights, shall be settled by arbitration under the rules of the International Chamber of Commerce (ICC). The arbitration shall take place in [City], [Country], and the language of the arbitration shall be English. The decision of the arbitrator(s) shall be final and binding on both parties.

This clause specifies arbitration as the dispute resolution method, defining the applicable rules, location and language.

Mediation is another effective approach, especially for disputes involving long-term business relationships. It allows the parties to work with a neutral mediator to reach a mutually acceptable agreement. Mediation is particularly useful in trademark cases, where disputes over similar names can be resolved with agreements that avoid confusion in the marketplace.

Direct trading is often the first step in intellectual property disputes. Parties can often resolve their differences without the need for third-party intervention, saving time and resources. Well-drafted contracts often include escalation clauses, which require parties to attempt to resolve disputes internally before pursuing ADRs or litigation.

In addition to these methods, technology is playing an increasing role in dispute resolution. Blockchain-based platforms are being used to provide immutable records of transactions and rights, helping to prove authorship and ownership in cases of infringement. These solutions can also automate parts of the resolution process, such as verifying digital contracts or tracking the use of protected assets.

Digital infringements, such as piracy and online counterfeiting, represent a growing area of concern for intellectual property. Below, a basic Python script demonstrates how a company can track unauthorized mentions of its brand on social media or websites:

python

```python
import requests
from bs4 import BeautifulSoup

def find_brand_mentions(brand, urls):
    """
    Check for mentions of a brand across multiple URLs.
    :param brand: str - The brand name to search for
    :param urls: list - List of URLs to search
    :return: dict - Dictionary of URLs and the number of mentions found
    """
    mentions = {}
    for url in urls:
```

```
    try:
        response = requests.get(url)
        if response.status_code == 200:
            content = response.text.lower()
            mentions[url] = content.count(brand.lower())
        else:
            mentions[url] = 0
    except requests.exceptions.RequestException as e:
        mentions[url] = f"Error: {e}"
    return mentions

brand_to_check = "protectedBrand"
websites = [
    "https://example1.com",
    "https://example2.com",
    "https://example3.com"
]

results = find_brand_mentions(brand_to_check, websites)
for site, count in results.items():
    print(f"{site}: {count} mentions")
```

This basic script tracks the number of mentions of a specific brand across multiple URLs, allowing companies to identify potential online infringements. An expanded version could include automatic notifications or integration with legal systems for immediate action.

In addition to technology, international collaboration is vital to dealing with transnational infringements. Organizations such as Interpol and the World Intellectual Property Organization (WIPO) promote initiatives to combat counterfeiting and piracy on a global scale. Programs like the Intellectual Property Rights Enforcement Network (IPR Enforcement Network) help coordinate efforts between countries to combat illicit activities.

Intellectual property disputes require a strategic approach that combines effective litigation with alternative resolution methods and the use of advanced technology. Companies operating globally must invest in continuous monitoring, collaboration with authorities and robust policies to protect their assets. In doing so, they ensure not only the protection of their rights, but also the integrity of their products and services in a competitive global marketplace.

CHAPTER 11: TECHNOLOGY TRANSFER

Technology transfer plays a key role in economic development and global innovation. It involves the dissemination of technical knowledge, skills, processes and products across organizations, countries and sectors. This transfer can occur in a variety of forms, including licensing, joint venture agreements, strategic partnerships, collaborative research, and foreign direct investment. In an interconnected global scenario, international technology transfer policies are essential to ensure that access to knowledge benefits both developed and emerging economies.

International technology transfer policies aim to balance encouraging innovation and promoting sustainable economic development. Treaties such as the TRIPS Agreement (Trade-Related Aspects of Intellectual Property Rights) establish guidelines to facilitate technology transfer between member countries of the World Trade Organization (WTO). Although TRIPS protects intellectual property rights, it also encourages developed countries to promote the dissemination of technology to developing economies.

Mechanisms such as compulsory licensing, included in TRIPS, allow governments to issue licenses for the production of technologies protected by patents without the authorization of the holder. This approach is often used in public health contexts, such as the production of generic medicines in low-income countries, to ensure access to essential treatments.

A notable example of successful technology transfer has occurred in the renewable energy sector. Developed countries, in partnership with emerging economies, have established programs to transfer solar and wind technologies. These agreements, often mediated by international organizations, have allowed developing nations to accelerate the implementation of clean energy, reduce dependence on fossil fuels, and create new industrial sectors.

The impact of technology transfer on developing economies is significant. It helps increase production capacity, improves global competitiveness and encourages local innovation. A practical case is the manufacturing sector in China, which has grown exponentially in recent decades, largely due to technology transfer from multinational companies. Investments in joint ventures with local companies allowed technical knowledge to be adapted and improved, resulting in a robust industrial base.

Despite the benefits, technology transfer faces challenges, especially related to the protection of intellectual property and the power imbalance between the parties involved. Multinational companies are often hesitant to share advanced technologies due to concerns about piracy and future competition. To overcome these barriers, detailed agreements that protect the rights of both parties are crucial.

Below is an example of a contractual clause for technology transfer that protects the interests of both parties:

text

Technology Transfer Agreement Clause:
The Licensor agrees to provide the Licensee with all necessary technical documentation, training, and support to implement the licensed technology. The Licensee shall not disclose, reproduce, or modify the transferred technology without prior written consent from the Licensor. Any improvements made to the technology by the Licensee during the term of this agreement shall be jointly owned by both parties, subject to further negotiation.

This clause ensures that the technology is used in a controlled manner and clearly defines the conditions for modifications or improvements.

Another important aspect of technology transfer is the role of universities and research institutions. Technological innovations often emerge in academic environments and are transferred to industry through public-private partnerships or business incubators. The technology transfer model in the United States, exemplified by the Bayh-Dole Act, allows academic institutions to retain intellectual property rights to government-funded innovations, encouraging the commercialization of scientific discoveries.

In developing economies, technology transfer can be a catalyst for the creation of entirely new industries. In the agriculture sector, technologies such as genetically modified seeds and advanced irrigation systems have been transferred to developing countries, resulting in increased productivity and food security.

The use of digital technology is also transforming technology transfer. Blockchain-based platforms are being used to track and authenticate technology transfer transactions, ensuring that intellectual property rights are respected. Below is an example Python script to simulate recording a technology transfer contract on a blockchain system:

python

```python
import hashlib
import datetime

class Blockchain:
    def __init__(self):
        self.chain = []
        self.create_block(previous_hash='0', data="Genesis Block")

    def create_block(self, previous_hash, data):
        block = {
            'index': len(self.chain) + 1,
```

```python
            'timestamp': str(datetime.datetime.now()),
            'date': date,
            'previous_hash': previous_hash,
            'hash': self.hash_block(data, previous_hash)
        }
        self.chain.append(block)
        return block

    @staticmethod
    def hash_block(data, previous_hash):
        to_hash = data + previous_hash + str(datetime.datetime.now())
        return hashlib.sha256(to_hash.encode()).hexdigest()

    def display_chain(self):
        for block in self.chain:
            print(block)

# Registering a technology transfer agreement
blockchain = Blockchain()
blockchain.create_block(previous_hash=blockchain.chain[-1]['hash'], data="Technology Transfer Agreement: Solar Panel Design")
blockchain.create_block(previous_hash=blockchain.chain[-1]['hash'], data="Training and Documentation Delivered")
blockchain.display_chain()
```

This script creates a blockchain ledger to track contracts and activities related to technology transfer. Each block represents a step in the process, ensuring integrity and traceability.

Governments play a vital role in encouraging technology transfer. Policies such as tax incentives for companies that share technologies with local partners and grants for collaborative research help facilitate the process. Furthermore, participation in global innovation networks, such as the Horizon Europe program, allows developing economies to access advanced technologies and finance research projects.

Technology transfer is a powerful tool for reducing global economic disparities and promoting sustainable development. However, it requires a delicate balance between protecting commercial interests and disseminating knowledge. With well-defined policies, clear agreements and the use of modern technology, technology transfer can continue to drive innovation and progress on a global scale.

CHAPTER 12: ARTIFICIAL INTELLIGENCE AND IP

The interplay between artificial intelligence (AI) and intellectual property (IP) represents one of the most challenging and innovative topics of the digital era. The ability of AIs to create original works, from music and text to algorithms and designs, raises fundamental questions about authorship, property rights, and the future of global regulation. As technology advances, IP needs to evolve to address the challenges and opportunities presented by AI.

Authorship of AI-Generated Works

One of the central issues in the debate about AI and IP is the definition of authorship. Traditionally, intellectual property rights are granted to individuals or entities who create something new and original. However, when an AI generates a work without significant human intervention, the question of who the author is becomes complex. There are different approaches to dealing with this situation:

1. **Programmer or Developer Recognition**: Some argue that the creators of the AI should be recognized as authors, since they were responsible for developing the system that generated the work.
2. **Authorship of the Operator or User**: Another perspective suggests that the user who instructed the AI to create the work should be considered the author, as he directed the creative process.
3. **Authored by AI itself**: In a more futuristic scenario, some proposals indicate that AI could be recognized as an author, although this would require significant

changes to current legislation, since non-human entities do not have legal rights.

The lack of consensus on these approaches reflects the different priorities of global jurisdictions. In the United States, for example, the Copyright Office has rejected protection for works created solely by AI, stating that copyright requires an element of human authorship. In the European Union, legislation emphasizes the need for creative human input, but remains open to future revision.

Practical Cases and Legal Implications

Case studies help illustrate the complexities associated with IP and AI. One notable situation involved a digital artist using an AI tool to generate a series of abstract images. After commercializing the works, the question arose as to who should own the copyright: the artist, the company that developed the tool or neither party, as the human element in the process was limited.

Another relevant example occurs in the music sector, where AIs are used to compose entire songs. A developer created an AI capable of composing melodies based on predefined musical styles. The generated songs were licensed for commercial use, but questions arose about how to divide the royalties between the developer, the AI operator and the end consumers who use these compositions.

These cases highlight the need for clear rules for assigning rights in contexts involving AI. The absence of guidelines can create legal uncertainty, making it difficult to protect and monetize AI-generated works.

Future Perspectives for Global Legislation

The future of IP and AI legislation will depend on coordinated efforts to balance the rights of AI creators, developers and users. Some proposals include:

1. **Creating Specific Categories for AI-Generated Works**:

Some jurisdictions may introduce a new category of intellectual property rights aimed at AI-generated works, with rules tailored to the nature of these creations.

2. **Regulation of Data Used for AI Training**: AI-generated works rely on large datasets used to train the models. Regulating the use of this data, especially if it is protected by copyright, will be essential to ensure that the works generated respect the rights of the original creators.

3. **Adoption of International Standards**: Harmonization of laws at a global level will be crucial to avoid conflicts of jurisdiction and facilitate the commercialization of AI-generated works in international markets.

4. **Recognition of Collaborative Models**: Often, AIs are used in collaboration with humans. Recognizing hybrid authoring models, where both the operator and the AI share credit, could be a viable solution.

Practical Applications of AI in IP

Beyond issues of authorship, AI is transforming the way IP rights are managed and enforced. AI-based tools are widely used to detect IP infringements such as piracy and trademark counterfeiting. Automated monitoring systems analyze large volumes of data to identify unauthorized content, offering rights holders a more efficient way to protect their creations.

Below is an example Python script that demonstrates how a basic tool can be configured to monitor potential copyright infringement online:

python

```
import requests
from bs4 import BeautifulSoup

def search_copyright_infringement(keyword, urls):
```

```
    """
    Search for potential copyright infringement based on a
keyword in a list of URLs.
    :param keyword: str - The keyword to search for (e.g., a title or
brand name)
    :param urls: list - A list of URLs to search
    :return: dict - Dictionary with URLs and infringement counts
    """
    results = {}
    for url in urls:
        try:
            response = requests.get(url)
            if response.status_code == 200:
                content = response.text.lower()
                results[url] = content.count(keyword.lower())
            else:
                results[url] = "Error fetching page"
        except Exception as e:
            results[url] = f"Error: {str(e)}"
    return results

urls_to_check = [
    "https://example.com/article1",
    "https://example.com/article2",
    "https://example.com/article3"
]

keyword_to_search = "ProtectedContent"

infringements =
search_copyright_infringement(keyword_to_search,
urls_to_check)
for site, count in infringements.items():
    print(f"{site}: {count} occurrences")
```

This basic script analyzes web pages for occurrences of a specific

keyword, such as the title of a copyrighted work. Although simplified, it can be integrated into larger systems for large-scale monitoring.

Economic and Cultural Impact

AI has the potential to democratize creation, allowing individuals without technical training to create high-quality works. However, this can also lead to an increase in the amount of content, making it difficult to differentiate between original and derivative works. Clear regulations can help balance accessibility and protection, encouraging both innovation and respect for existing rights.

Ethical Considerations

In addition to legal issues, the use of AI in the creation of intellectual works raises ethical considerations. Who should be responsible for AI-generated content that infringes existing rights or disseminates misleading information? Regulations need to address these concerns, ensuring that AI is used responsibly.

The integration of AI and IP represents a unique opportunity to reshape the concept of creation and innovation. As legislation evolves, it will be essential to consider the technical, legal and ethical complexities of this relationship, ensuring that benefits are widely distributed and that the rights of everyone involved are respected.

CHAPTER 13: STRATEGIC IP MANAGEMENT

Strategic intellectual property (IP) management is an indispensable practice for organizations seeking to maximize the value of their intangible assets in global markets. With increasing dependence on innovative technologies, strong brands and unique designs, companies need to adopt structured strategies to protect, manage and monetize their intellectual creations. The valuation of IP assets, combined with advanced management tools, allows multinational companies to gain competitive advantages and increase their market presence.

Asset Valuation in Global Contexts

IP assets such as patents, trademarks, copyrights and trade secrets are often an organization's most valuable elements. Valuing these assets is essential for a range of purposes, including mergers and acquisitions, licensing, financing, tax planning and dispute resolution. However, determining the value of intangible assets requires methodological approaches that take into account economic, technological and legal factors.

Three main methods are used to value IP assets:

1. **Cost Method**: Evaluates the historical cost or replacement cost of an asset. This method is most appropriate for assets such as internally developed software or databases.
2. **Income Method**: It is based on the present value of expected future cash flows generated by the asset. For example, a patent that guarantees market exclusivity may be valued based on projected revenue during its term.

3. **Market Method**: Compares the asset with similar asset transactions under market conditions. This method is often used to evaluate brands, considering the brand's reputation and recognition in the market.

The practical application of these methods can be observed in cases such as the licensing of electric vehicle technologies. A company that develops advanced batteries can estimate the value of its patent using the income method, calculating future revenue from royalties paid by automakers that license the technology.

Furthermore, the valuation of IP assets in global contexts must take into account regional differences in regulations, market competition and potential legal risks. For example, a global brand may have different values in different regions due to cultural, economic and social factors.

Management Tools for Multinationals

Effective IP asset management requires robust tools that allow you to monitor, protect and optimize a company's intellectual property portfolio. Multinational organizations often face unique challenges due to the size and complexity of their operations, but modern technologies offer powerful solutions to overcome these difficulties.

1. **Intellectual Property Management Systems (IPMS)**
   IPMS software centralizes information related to a company's IP portfolio, allowing the monitoring of registrations, renewals, litigation and licenses. Tools like Anaqua, CPA Global and PatSnap offer functionality including portfolio analysis, competitor monitoring and reporting.
2. **Offender Monitoring**
   Automated systems help companies identify IP violations in global markets. Algorithms based on artificial intelligence crawl marketplaces, websites and social networks to identify counterfeit products or

unauthorized content. A practical example of Python code that can be used for basic monitoring of brands on marketplaces is below:

python

```
import requests
from bs4 import BeautifulSoup

def monitor_marketplace(brand_name, marketplace_url):
    """
    Monitor a marketplace for potential trademark infringements.
    :param brand_name: str - The brand name to search for
    :param marketplace_url: str - URL of the marketplace
    :return: list - List of product listings mentioning the brand
name
    """
    try:
        response = requests.get(marketplace_url)
        if response.status_code == 200:
            soup = BeautifulSoup(response.content, "html.parser")
            listings = soup.find_all("div", class_="product-listing")  #
Example class
            infringements = [listing.text for listing in listings if
brand_name.lower() in listing.text.lower()]
            return infringements
        else:
            print("Failed to fetch marketplace data.")
            return []
    except Exception as e:
        print(f"Error: {e}")
        return []

marketplace = "https://examplemarketplace.com"
brand = "ProtectedBrand"

infringing_listings = monitor_marketplace(brand, marketplace)
```

```
if infringing_listings:
    print("Potential infringements detected:")
    for listing in infringing_listings:
        print(listing)
else:
    print("No infringements found.")
```

This script scans listings on a marketplace to detect possible unauthorized uses of a trademark. More advanced systems would integrate automatic notifications and trend analysis.

3. **Licensing and Contract Management**
   License management is a critical part of IP monetization. Contract management tools allow companies to track royalty payments, enforce contract clauses, and ensure compliance with licensing terms. Software such as ContraxSuite and Ironclad automate these processes, reducing errors and optimizing administration.

4. **Scenario Projection and Simulation**
   Predictive analytics tools help companies evaluate what-if scenarios, such as the impact of a new patent on the market or the risks of entering a new jurisdiction. These systems use big data and machine learning to provide strategic insights.

Strategic IP Integration in Multinationals

For IP management to be truly strategic, it must be integrated with broader corporate objectives. This includes aligning the IP portfolio with research and development initiatives, market planning and global expansion. Leading companies often create dedicated IP departments, led by specialized executives, who work closely with legal, marketing and R&D teams.

Additionally, collaboration with local IP offices and international organizations is essential to ensure that assets are protected in all relevant jurisdictions. Ongoing employee training programs help reinforce a culture of awareness of the importance of IP at all levels of the organization.

Practical Examples of Success

Companies like IBM, Samsung and Procter & Gamble illustrate how strategic IP management can generate impressive results. IBM, for example, is consistently one of the largest patent holders in the world. Its approach includes identifying strategic areas for innovation, licensing technologies to generate revenue and using its patents as leverage in commercial negotiations.

In the consumer goods sector, Procter & Gamble uses its extensive trademark base to build consumer loyalty and differentiate its products in saturated markets. The company also employs licensing strategies to expand the reach of its brands into new territories.

Strategic IP management is an essential competency for organizations operating in a globalized economic scenario. With modern tools and well-structured practices, companies can protect their assets, explore new market opportunities and maximize the return on investments in innovation. The combination of accurate valuation, advanced technology and corporate integration ensures that IP is not just a legal asset, but also an engine of growth and competitiveness.

CHAPTER 14: IP IN THE CREATIVE INDUSTRY

Intellectual property (IP) plays an essential role in the creative industry, covering sectors such as fashion, audiovisual, music and games. These sectors depend on innovation and originality to thrive, making IP protection crucial to encourage creativity, secure revenues and combat practices such as piracy and counterfeiting. Effective IP management in these fields not only protects creators, but also promotes a healthy business environment, stimulating economic and cultural growth.

Impacts of IP on Fashion

The fashion sector is characterized by a constant renewal of designs, patterns and trends. IP provides a framework to protect these elements and prevent unique creations from being copied by competitors. Industrial design protection is widely used in fashion to ensure that clothing, shoes, bags and accessories are protected against imitations.

In addition to industrial designs, trademarks play a central role in the fashion industry. A strong trademark not only differentiates products but also adds emotional value to consumers. Big fashion brands, such as Chanel, Gucci and Nike, invest heavily in protecting their logos, slogans and visual identity.

Piracy is one of the biggest challenges facing fashion. Counterfeit products, which often imitate luxury designs and brands, can damage companies' reputations and generate significant financial losses. To combat this, brands are adopting innovative technologies, such as blockchain, to authenticate products. A QR code linked to a blockchain system, for example, could allow consumers to verify the authenticity of a luxury handbag before purchasing it.

Audiovisual e PI

The audiovisual industry, which includes films, TV shows and online videos, relies heavily on copyright to protect scripts, productions and soundtracks. Copyright ensures that creators are rewarded for the use of their works, whether through sales, exhibitions or broadcasts.

A practical example of the application of IP in audiovisual is the distribution of films on streaming platforms. Services like Netflix and Disney+ operate with strictly controlled licenses, which determine where and how content can be displayed. These licenses ensure that creators and studios are adequately compensated for the use of their works.

Digital piracy continues to be a significant challenge for audiovisual. Films and series are often made available on pirated websites shortly after their release, harming producers' profits. To deal with this, companies use advanced detection and removal systems, which identify and eliminate illegal copies on the internet. A basic Python script can be employed to monitor suspicious websites and identify copies of protected content:

python

```
import requests
from bs4 import BeautifulSoup

def monitor_piracy(content_title, websites):
    """
    Monitor websites for pirated copies of a specific content title.
    :param content_title: str - The title of the content to search for
    :param websites: list - A list of websites to monitor
    :return: dict - Dictionary of websites and piracy mentions
    """
    results = {}
    for website in websites:
```

```
        try:
            response = requests.get(website)
            if response.status_code == 200:
                soup = BeautifulSoup(response.content,
"html.parser")
                if content_title.lower() in soup.text.lower():
                    results[website] = "Pirated content detected"
                else:
                    results[website] = "No piracy detected"
            else:
                results[website] = "Website unavailable"
        except Exception as e:
            results[website] = f"Error: {str(e)}"
    return results

content_to_monitor = "Popular Movie Title"
websites_to_check = [
    "https://examplepiratesite.com",
    "https://anotherpiratesite.com"
]

piracy_results = monitor_piracy(content_to_monitor,
websites_to_check)
for site, status in piracy_results.items():
    print(f"{site}: {status}")
```

This script searches suspicious websites for a specific title, helping companies quickly identify violations and take legal action.

Music and IP

In the music sector, copyright is the main protection mechanism. They ensure that songwriters, lyricists, and artists receive royalties for the use of their music. Digital distribution has revolutionized music, making platforms like Spotify, Apple Music and YouTube key players in the sector's economy.

However, digital piracy and the unauthorized use of music in user-created content are ongoing challenges. Tools like YouTube's Content ID help detect protected music in videos uploaded to the platform, allowing rights holders to monetize or block content.

The collaboration between technology and IP in music can also be seen in the use of NFTs (non-fungible tokens). Artists have used NFTs to sell exclusive tracks, digital tickets and personalized experiences directly to fans, creating new sources of revenue and engagement.

Games e PI

The games industry is one of the most profitable and innovative creative sectors. Games involve a combination of IP-protected elements, including software, character designs, soundtracks, and storylines. Protecting these elements is essential to ensure developers can recoup their investments and continue innovating.

Game piracy, whether through illegal downloads or software modifications (cracking), is a recurring problem. Companies like Ubisoft and EA use advanced DRM (digital rights management) systems to protect their games against unauthorized copies. These systems limit access to content to licensed users only.

An interesting example of IP innovation in games is the use of artificial intelligence to generate dynamic content. Games that use AI to create unique worlds or adapt gameplay in real time raise questions about who owns the copyright to these generated elements. Future regulation will need to address these issues to protect both developers and players.

Examples of Successful Protection

1. **Hermès and the Design of Bags**: Hermès protected the iconic design of its Birkin bag from copycats by trademarking the bag's appearance as an industrial design. This allowed the company to sue copycat manufacturers and preserve the market value of the product.

2. **Disney and Character Copyrights**: Disney is known for its strict approach to protecting characters like Mickey Mouse and Elsa. The company uses a combination of copyrights, trademarks, and licensing agreements to protect its creations.

3. **Spotify and Music Licensing**: Spotify revolutionized music distribution by implementing a licensing model that pays royalties directly to rights holders for each playback. This reduced dependence on physical CDs and combatted piracy.

4. **Epic Games e o Fortnite**: Epic Games protected the character designs, game mechanics, and even popular dances used in Fortnite, ensuring that other companies could not replicate these elements without authorization.

IP in the creative industry is an essential driver for innovation and economic growth. Effectively managing these rights ensures that creators and companies can continue producing high-quality content, while technological tools help combat piracy and protect creative assets. With solid strategies and clear regulations, IP will continue to play a vital role in the success of the creative industry in a globalized market.

CHAPTER 15: IP AND HEALTH

The interaction between intellectual property (IP) and health is a complex topic that involves economic, ethical, political and technological issues. Pharmaceutical patents, in particular, play a crucial role in advancing medicine, allowing companies to recoup significant investments in research and development (R&D). However, these same patents can limit access to essential medicines, especially in low- and middle-income countries, raising debates about social justice, equity and the role of international legislation.

Pharmaceutical Patents and Drug Development

Patents are fundamental to the pharmaceutical sector. They guarantee market exclusivity for a limited period, usually 20 years, allowing companies to recover high R&D costs. It is estimated that developing a new drug can cost billions of dollars and take more than a decade to complete. Patents encourage this investment by protecting innovations against copying by competitors during the exclusivity period.

The exclusivity provided by patents is also essential for financing clinical studies, which are rigorous and expensive. These studies are carried out in several phases to ensure the safety and effectiveness of new medicines before their approval by regulatory bodies, such as the FDA (Food and Drug Administration) in the United States or the EMA (European Medicines Agency) in the European Union.

An emblematic example of innovation protected by patents is the development of antiviral drugs for the treatment of HIV. Pharmaceutical companies invested massively in creating effective therapies, and patents gave these companies the time needed to recoup their initial costs. After the exclusivity period ended, generic medicines began to be produced, making treatments more accessible around the world.

Global Access and Compulsory Licensing

Although patents are essential for innovation, they can limit access to medicines, especially in developing countries. High prices for patented medicines often make them inaccessible to vulnerable populations, creating significant barriers to public health.

Compulsory licensing is a mechanism that allows governments to authorize the production of generic medicines without the permission of the patent holder. This measure is provided for in the TRIPS Agreement (Trade-Related Aspects of Intellectual Property Rights), administered by the World Trade Organization (WTO). Compulsory licensing is generally used in public health emergency situations, such as epidemics.

A relevant case was India's use of compulsory licensing to allow the production of a generic cancer drug that was inaccessible due to its high cost. The measure drastically reduced the price of the medicine, expanding access for thousands of patients. However, this practice has also generated controversy, with pharmaceutical companies arguing that compulsory licensing discourages innovation.

Ethical and Political Debates

Debates about IP and healthcare often revolve around ethical and political issues. One of the most discussed points is the balance between the rights of innovators and public health needs. While pharmaceutical companies defend strict patent protection as an incentive for innovation, health activists argue that access to essential medicines should be treated as a human right.

The COVID-19 pandemic has highlighted the importance of these debates. The race to develop effective vaccines has led to an increase in the use of licensing agreements and public-private partnerships to speed up production and distribution. However, questions about equity in access to vaccines quickly emerged. High-income countries secured most of the initial vaccine supply, while many low-income countries faced shortages.

International organizations such as the WHO have pushed for technology sharing mechanisms such as C-TAP (COVID-19 Technology Access Pool) to enable voluntary licensing of COVID-19 related technologies. This initiative aimed to increase global production of vaccines and treatments, but faced resistance from some companies and governments.

Technological Tools for Patent Management

Technology is playing an increasingly important role in pharmaceutical patent management. Patent search and analysis systems help companies and governments identify relevant patents, predict market trends, and plan licensing strategies.

An example of the use of technology in the context of IP is the monitoring of patent expirations, allowing generic manufacturers to plan their operations. The script below demonstrates how to create a simple tool to track basic patent information using public APIs:

```python
import requests

def get_patent_details(patent_number):
    """
    Retrieve details about a specific patent using a public API.
    :param patent_number: str - The patent number to search for
    :return: dict - Details about the patent
    """
    url = f"https://api.patentsview.org/patents/{patent_number}"
    try:
        response = requests.get(url)
        if response.status_code == 200:
```

```
            return response.json()
        else:
            return {"error": f"Unable to retrieve details for patent
{patent_number}"}
    except Exception as e:
        return {"error": str(e)}

patent_number = "US12345678"
patent_info = get_patent_details(patent_number)
print(patent_info)
```

This basic script can be integrated into larger systems to monitor patent portfolios and analyze data at scale.

The Role of International Organizations

Organizations such as the WHO, WTO and UNAIDS play important roles in mediating between commercial interests and public health needs. They promote policies that encourage the sharing of knowledge and technology, especially in critical areas such as vaccines and medicines for neglected diseases.

Collaboration between governments, NGOs and businesses is essential to ensure the IP system is fair and equitable. Initiatives like the Global Fund have shown how global partnerships can finance and distribute essential medicines in low-income countries, saving millions of lives.

Future of IP and Health

As new technologies such as artificial intelligence and biotechnology transform healthcare, the role of IP will continue to evolve. Personalizing medicine, for example, may require new approaches to protecting and sharing innovations. Similarly, AI, used to develop medicines, raises questions about the authorship and ownership of machine-generated creations.

In the future, healthcare IP will need to find ways to balance innovation and accessibility. Flexible licensing models, global partnerships and the use of advanced technology can help achieve this balance, ensuring that the benefits of innovation reach everyone who needs them, regardless of their location or economic status.

CHAPTER 16: INTELLECTUAL PROPERTY AND SUSTAINABILITY

Intellectual property (IP) plays an essential role in promoting sustainability by providing incentives for the development and dissemination of innovative technologies that address global environmental challenges. As awareness of the need for sustainable practices grows, the IP system has adapted to support green innovations, protecting inventors' ideas and encouraging investment in solutions that contribute to a more sustainable future.

Incentives for Green Innovation

Green innovation encompasses a wide range of technologies and practices designed to reduce environmental impact, improve energy efficiency and promote the sustainable use of natural resources. From wind turbines and solar panels to circular economy systems, sustainable innovation requires significant financial and intellectual resources. IP offers protection mechanisms that allow inventors to obtain a return on their investments, encouraging the creation of new solutions.

Governments and international organizations have taken specific measures to encourage green innovation through patents and other IP rights. Some of these measures include:

1. **Fast-Track Patents**
   Several patent offices, such as the European Patent Office (EPO) and the United States Patent and Trademark Office (USPTO), offer priority examination programs for patents related to sustainable technologies. These programs allow inventors to obtain legal protection more quickly, encouraging the development and

commercialization of green innovations.

2. **Subsidies and Tax Incentives**

   Many countries offer subsidies and tax incentives for projects that promote sustainability. Companies that file patents related to green technologies can qualify for additional financial benefits, reducing the cost of development and encouraging research.

3. **Shared Licensing and Open Source**

   To accelerate the dissemination of sustainable technologies, some inventors and companies choose to license their innovations through open models or at reduced rates. Initiatives such as Eco-Patent Commons promote the sharing of patents related to green solutions, allowing other companies to use these technologies to expand their positive environmental impact.

Success Stories in Sustainable Technologies

The success stories highlight how IP has contributed to the advancement of sustainable technologies across different sectors, including energy, transport, agriculture and manufacturing.

1. Renewable Energy

Renewable energy is one of the sectors most impacted by IP. Companies like Tesla and Vestas have used patents to protect innovations in high-capacity batteries and next-generation wind turbines, respectively. These technologies have helped reduce the cost of clean energy and increase its global accessibility.

Tesla, for example, released its electric vehicle patents in 2014 to encourage competition and accelerate the transition to sustainable transportation. This strategic decision highlighted the importance of balancing IP rights with the need for collaboration on technologies critical to sustainability.

2. Sustainable Agriculture

In the agricultural sector, IP protects innovations such as genetically modified seeds that increase productivity and reduce the use of pesticides. Companies like Bayer and Syngenta have invested in technologies that help farmers use less water and fertilizers, promoting more sustainable agricultural practices.

3. Circular Economy

The circular economy, which seeks to minimize waste and maximize the use of resources, also benefits from IP. Startups and large companies are developing innovative recycling processes, such as transforming plastics into new materials. These processes are protected by patents, allowing inventors to monetize their innovations while helping to reduce environmental impact.

Below is a practical example of how digital technology can be used to monitor and optimize recycling processes:

python

```python
import random

def optimize_recycling_process(material, quantity):
    """
    Optimize recycling processes based on material type and
quantity.
    :param material: str - The type of material (e.g., "plastic",
"metal")
    :param quantity: int - Quantity of material in kilograms
    :return: dict - Suggested recycling method and estimated
efficiency
    """
    recycling_methods = {
        "plastic": {"method": "chemical recycling", "efficiency":
random.uniform(80, 95)},
        "metal": {"method": "smelting", "efficiency":
random.uniform(90, 99)},
        "glass": {"method": "melting and reshaping", "efficiency":
random.uniform(85, 97)}
    }
    if material.lower() in recycling_methods:
```

```
        method = recycling_methods[material.lower()]
        return {
            "material": material,
            "quantity": quantity,
            "suggested_method": method["method"],
            "estimated_efficiency": f"{method['efficiency']:.2f}%"
        }
    else:
        return {"error": "Material not supported for optimization"}

# Example usage
material_type = "plastic"
material_quantity = 500  # in kilograms

optimized_process = optimize_recycling_process(material_type,
material_quantity)
print(optimized_process)
```

This code provides suggestions on recycling methods based on the type and quantity of material, helping to improve the efficiency and sustainability of processes.

4. Sustainable Transport

The transport sector has also been a major beneficiary of IP in sustainability. Innovations such as high-speed trains, electric public transport systems and hydrogen technologies are protected by patents that encourage continued development and large-scale adoption.

Challenges and Solutions

Although IP offers significant incentives for green innovation, challenges remain. The high cost of developing sustainable technologies can make access difficult for startups and smaller companies. Furthermore, strict IP protection can create barriers to sharing technologies in regions that need them most.

Solutions to these challenges include:

- **Public-Private Partnerships**: Collaborations between governments, companies and non-governmental organizations can finance and promote the sharing of green technologies.
- **Global IP Sharing Policies**: Initiatives such as the Paris Agreement can be complemented with guidelines on sharing sustainable innovations, ensuring that critical technologies are accessible globally.
- **Education and Training**: Promoting awareness about the role of IP in sustainability can help inventors and companies better navigate the system and harness its benefits.

IP plays a crucial role in advancing sustainability by encouraging innovations that address global environmental challenges. As green technologies continue to evolve, balancing rights protection and access to innovations will be essential to maximize environmental, social and economic benefits. With well-structured policies and strategic collaborations, IP can become a powerful tool to drive the global transition to a more sustainable future.

CHAPTER 17: IP AND TRADITIONAL KNOWLEDGE

The protection of traditional knowledge and indigenous knowledge within the intellectual property (IP) system is one of the biggest challenges facing the international community. This knowledge, often transmitted orally for generations, plays a crucial role in preserving biodiversity, in innovation in areas such as health and agriculture, and in strengthening cultural identities. However, the unauthorized commercial exploitation of these resources, often called biopiracy, has led to intense debates about justice, rights and sovereignty.

Protection of Indigenous Knowledge

Traditional knowledge encompasses practices, knowledge, skills and innovations developed by indigenous and local communities. This knowledge is often linked to the sustainable use of natural resources and the in-depth understanding of specific ecosystems. Examples include herbal medicines, agricultural methods adapted to extreme weather conditions, and spiritual and cultural practices.

However, unlike traditional forms of IP, such as patents or trademarks, traditional knowledge rarely fits conventional protection criteria. These criteria generally require novelty and individual authorship, whereas indigenous knowledge often involves collective contributions and a history of continued use.

To deal with these particularities, several international initiatives have sought to adapt the IP system to recognize and protect the rights of indigenous communities. One of the most effective strategies is the use of **traditional knowledge databases**, which record information formally to avoid misappropriation.

Biopiracy and Legal Challenges

Biopiracy refers to the exploitation or appropriation of biological resources and traditional knowledge without the consent of the communities that developed or maintain them. This includes cases where companies or institutions register patents based on indigenous resources or practices without sharing benefits or recognizing the rights of communities.

A notorious example of biopiracy was the case of the patent on neem, a plant widely used in India for its medicinal and agricultural properties. International companies have registered patents for neem extracts, which has generated legal controversy and led to the annulment of some of these patents, highlighting the need to protect traditional knowledge.

Another case involved the use of genes from Basmati rice, a traditional variety grown in India and Pakistan. The patent issued to a foreign company sparked international protests and debates over how to protect traditional agricultural varieties from appropriation.

International Conventions: Nagoya Protocol

THE **Nagoya Protocol on Access to Genetic Resources and Fair and Equitable Sharing of Benefits Derived from Their Use (ABS)**, adopted in 2010 under the Convention on Biological Diversity (CBD), is one of the main international instruments to deal with the protection of traditional knowledge and combat biopiracy.

The protocol establishes clear guidelines for the use of genetic resources and associated knowledge, ensuring that the communities that provide these resources are consulted and receive fair benefits. The protocol's core principles include:

1. **Prior Informed Consent (PIC)**
   Before accessing genetic resources or traditional knowledge, users must obtain the consent of the communities that hold them. This ensures that

communities have the power to decide how their knowledge is used.

2. **Mutually Agreed Terms (MAT)**
   The benefits derived from the use of genetic resources must be negotiated on terms mutually agreed between the parties, covering both financial and non-financial benefits, such as technology transfer and capacity building.

3. **Monitoring and Compliance**
   Member countries must implement monitoring mechanisms to ensure that the principles of the protocol are respected, including the creation of checkpoints to verify compliance.

Digital Tools for Protecting Traditional Knowledge

Digital technology is playing an increasing role in protecting traditional knowledge, enabling indigenous communities and governments to record and monitor knowledge effectively. Databases, blockchain and artificial intelligence are some of the tools that can be used to ensure that this knowledge is protected against misappropriation.

Below is an example of how blockchain can be applied to record and track the use of traditional knowledge:

python

```python
import hashlib
import datetime

class TraditionalKnowledgeBlockchain:
    def __init__(self):
        self.chain = []
        self.create_block(previous_hash='0', data="Genesis Block")

    def create_block(self, previous_hash, data):
        block = {
            'index': len(self.chain) + 1,
```

```
        'timestamp': str(datetime.datetime.now()),
        'date': date,
        'previous_hash': previous_hash,
        'hash': self.hash_block(data, previous_hash)
    }
    self.chain.append(block)
    return block

@staticmethod
def hash_block(data, previous_hash):
    to_hash = data + previous_hash +
str(datetime.datetime.now())
        return hashlib.sha256(to_hash.encode()).hexdigest()

def display_chain(self):
    for block in self.chain:
        print(block)

# Registering traditional knowledge
blockchain = TraditionalKnowledgeBlockchain()
blockchain.create_block(previous_hash=blockchain.chain[-1]
['hash'], data="Medicinal plant knowledge: Neem")
blockchain.create_block(previous_hash=blockchain.chain[-1]
['hash'], data="Agricultural practice: Rice terracing technique")
blockchain.display_chain()
```

This code demonstrates how to use blockchain to record information about traditional knowledge, creating an immutable and traceable record that can be used to protect that knowledge from undue exploitation.

Success Stories in Protecting Traditional Knowledge

1. **Indian Traditional Knowledge Database**
   India has created a digital database called Traditional Knowledge Digital Library (TKDL) to record traditional knowledge in areas such as Ayurvedic medicine and

agricultural practices. This database has been integrated into patent search systems in several jurisdictions, helping to prevent the registration of inappropriate patents.

2. **Nagoya Protocol in Brazil**
Brazil implemented the Nagoya Protocol to protect the biodiversity of the Amazon and the associated knowledge of indigenous communities. Brazilian regulations require companies to obtain prior consent and share benefits when using genetic resources or traditional knowledge.

3. **Training in African Countries**
Several African countries, such as Kenya and South Africa, have implemented capacity building programs to help local communities protect their knowledge and negotiate fair terms with companies seeking access to these resources.

Challenges and Opportunities

Although significant advances have been made in protecting traditional knowledge, challenges remain. The lack of formal documentation, inequality of power in negotiations and gaps in regulatory enforcement make it difficult to effectively protect this knowledge.

On the other hand, opportunities for integration of digital technologies, increased international collaboration, and greater global awareness offer promising paths to address these challenges. Governments, international organizations and businesses have a crucial role to play in creating a system that respects and protects the rights of indigenous communities while promoting sustainable innovation.

IP and the protection of traditional knowledge are fundamental to ensuring justice and equity in an interconnected world. With the support of international conventions such as the Nagoya Protocol, advanced technologies and collaboration between interested parties, it is possible to protect knowledge that is the legacy of generations and an invaluable resource for the future of the planet.

CHAPTER 18: IP IN STARTUPS

Intellectual property (IP) is one of the most valuable assets for startups operating in emerging markets. From protecting technological innovations to building strong brands, IP plays a strategic role in the growth and scalability of these companies. Startups often face unique challenges such as limited resources and high competition, which makes it essential to adopt effective strategies to manage and protect their IP assets.

Strategies for Startups in Emerging Markets

Startups in emerging markets face challenging contexts, including inconsistent regulations, competition from established companies, and the need to attract investors. IP can be a powerful tool for overcoming these barriers by providing legal protection, creating market differentiation and increasing the value perceived by investors.

1. Identification of IP Assets

The first step to an effective IP strategy is to identify the intangible assets that the startup has. These assets may include:

- **Patents**: Technological innovations or unique processes.
- **Brands**: Names, logos and slogans that differentiate the company in the market.
- **Copyright**: Original content, such as software, designs, or marketing materials.
- **Trade Secrets**: Confidential business formulas, algorithms or strategies.

Clearly identifying these assets allows the startup to prioritize which ones to protect based on their strategic impact.

2. Registration and Protection of IP Rights

Once identified, IP assets must be registered on relevant markets. Registration guarantees legal protection against unauthorized use and facilitates the marketing of products or services.

- **Patents**: Startups must carefully evaluate which innovations are eligible for patents. In emerging markets, where costs can be a limiting factor, startups may choose to protect patents only in priority markets.
- **Brands**: Registering trademarks is crucial to avoid name disputes and protect the company's identity.
- **Trade Secrets**: Implementing non-disclosure agreements (NDAs) with employees and partners helps protect trade secrets from leaks.

3. Monitoring of Competitors and Infringers

Startups should regularly monitor markets to identify potential infringers of their IP rights. Tools based on artificial intelligence and digital tracking can be used for this purpose.

Below is an example of Python code that can be used to track online listings that misuse a trademark:

python

```python
import requests
from bs4 import BeautifulSoup

def monitor_brand_infringement(brand_name, urls):
    """
    Monitor websites for unauthorized use of a brand name.
    :param brand_name: str - The brand name to search for
    :param urls: list - List of URLs to monitor
    :return: dict - Dictionary of URLs and infringement
occurrences
    """
    results = {}
    for url in urls:
        try:
```

```
        response = requests.get(url)
        if response.status_code == 200:
            content = response.text.lower()
            occurrences = content.count(brand_name.lower())
            results[url] = occurrences if occurrences > 0 else "No
infringement detected"
        else:
            results[url] = "Failed to access"
    except Exception as e:
        results[url] = f"Error: {str(e)}"
    return results

brand = "InnovativeStartup"
websites_to_check = [
    "https://example1.com",
    "https://example2.com"
]

infringement_results = monitor_brand_infringement(brand,
websites_to_check)
for site, result in infringement_results.items():
    print(f"{site}: {result}")
```

This script checks whether a brand name appears on specific websites, helping startups identify potential IP infringements.

4. Licensing and Monetization

IP not only protects a startup's innovations, but can also be a source of revenue. Licensing patents or trademarks to other companies allows startups to monetize their assets while expanding their market influence.

5. Attracting Investments

Investors are increasingly paying attention to IP as an indicator of value and innovation. A well-structured IP portfolio can increase a startup's valuation by providing concrete evidence of its ability to innovate and protect its ideas.

Examples of Protection and Scalability

1. Payments Technology in Emerging Markets

A startup in an emerging market has developed a mobile payments solution that allows internet-free transactions. To protect the innovation, the company registered a patent that covers both the algorithm and the hardware used. This IP asset made the startup attractive to investors and facilitated partnerships with banks and telephone operators.

2. Brand Identity in the Fashion Sector

A sustainable fashion startup in an emerging market has built its brand with a focus on products made from recycled materials. By trademarking its exclusive brand and designs, the company avoided copying and reinforced its appeal as a trusted brand. The brand value also allowed the startup to scale its operations to international markets.

3. Software as a Service (SaaS) for Agriculture

A startup that developed a SaaS platform for agricultural data management has copyrighted its software and patented its unique algorithms. This protection helped the company avoid direct competition and attract farmers in emerging markets who needed affordable solutions.

Technological Solutions for Startups

Digital tools are becoming indispensable for startups to manage and protect their IP. Some of these solutions include:

- **PI Management Systems (IPMS)**: Software like Anaqua and PatSnap help startups monitor renewal deadlines, manage licenses, and track competitors.
- **Blockchain for Intellectual Property**: Startups can use blockchain to record innovations, creating immutable records that serve as proof of authorship.
- **Collaboration Platforms**: Tools like DocuSign and Adobe Sign allow startups to sign NDAs and IP agreements

digitally, ensuring security and compliance.

IP is a strategic asset that can drive the growth of startups in emerging markets. From protecting innovations to creating new revenue streams, effective IP management enables startups to navigate challenging markets with confidence. With the integration of modern technologies and well-defined strategies, startups can maximize the value of their intangible assets and establish solid foundations for long-term success.

CHAPTER 19: IP IN EDUCATION AND RESEARCH

Intellectual property (IP) plays a central role in education and research, promoting the creation, dissemination and protection of knowledge. The academic environment is one of the biggest generators of innovation, from scientific publications to technological discoveries that shape entire industries. IP provides the legal framework necessary to protect these innovations, encourage collaboration between institutions and ensure that the benefits of knowledge are shared fairly.

Rights over Academic Publications

Academic publications represent one of the most common forms of intellectual results generated by researchers. These publications are protected by copyright, which guarantees the author control over the use, distribution and reproduction of their work. However, the complexities of the academic system, such as relationships with publishers and open access mandates, create unique challenges for managing rights over academic publications.

1. Copyright in Academic Publications

Authors of scientific articles often transfer the copyright of their works to academic publishers as a condition of publication. This limits the author's control over their research, including their ability to share the content with the academic community. To mitigate these limitations, many universities and researchers choose to publish under open access licenses, such as Creative Commons licenses, which allow for more flexible use of content.

Below is an example of how Creative Commons licenses can be

used to protect and share academic publications:

text

This approach ensures that authors maintain part of their rights while promoting free access to knowledge.

2. Open Access Mandates

Research institutions and funders are increasingly adopting open access mandates, requiring that the results of publicly funded research be made freely available. Platforms like PubMed Central and arXiv play an important role in fulfilling these mandates, allowing researchers to publish their works in an accessible way while maintaining copyright.

3. Rights Management in Academic Collaborations

Academic research often involves collaborations between multiple institutions, making IP rights management a critical aspect. Clear contracts that define intellectual property, publishing responsibilities and benefit sharing are essential to avoid future conflicts.

Technology Transfer in Universities

Technology transfer is the process of transforming academic innovations into marketable products, services or processes. This process involves protecting innovations, negotiating licensing agreements and collaborating with companies to bring technologies to market.

1. Technology Transfer Offices (TTOs)

Universities often establish technology transfer offices (TTOs) to manage the commercialization process. TTOs perform several roles, including:

- **Assessment of Inventions**: Determine the commercial potential of academic discoveries.
- **IP Protection**: Register patents, trademarks or copyrights to protect innovations.
- **Licensing**: Negotiate licensing agreements with companies that wish to use the technology.
- **Startup Creation**: Support the formation of startups based on university technologies.

Below is an example of how a licensing agreement might be structured for a technology developed at a university:

text

Technology Licensing Agreement
1. Parties: This agreement is between [University Name] (Licensor) and [Company Name] (Licensee).
2. License Grant: The Licensor grants the Licensee a non-exclusive license to use the patented technology for the purpose of manufacturing and selling [product description].
3. Royalties: The Licensee agrees to pay a royalty of [percentage] on net sales of the product.
4. Term: This agreement is effective for a period of [number] years from the date of execution.
5. Confidentiality: The Licensee agrees to maintain the confidentiality of all proprietary information related to the technology.
6. Termination: The Licensor reserves the right to terminate the agreement in case of breach of terms by the Licensee.

This model establishes the basic conditions for a company to use protected technology, encouraging innovation while guaranteeing benefits for the university.

2. Incentives for Researchers

To encourage researchers to participate in the technology transfer process, many universities offer financial benefits and professional recognition. This could include a percentage of royalties generated by licensed technologies or institutional support to turn ideas into startups.

3. Examples of Successful Technology Transfer

Google: The Google search engine was based on a research project developed at Stanford University. The university licensed the technology to the company's founders, generating significant returns.

CRISPR: CRISPR gene editing technology was developed at several academic institutions, including UC Berkeley and MIT. Technology transfer has resulted in partnerships and licenses with pharmaceutical and biotechnology companies.

Technological Solutions for IP Management in Education and Research

IP management in academia is benefiting from digital tools that simplify complex processes. Some solutions include:

- **Invention Management Systems**: Platforms that allow researchers to register innovations and track their protection and commercialization status.
- **Blockchain for IP Traceability**: Universities can use blockchain to create immutable records of discoveries, making it easier to track copyrights and patents.
- **Collaboration Platforms**: Tools like DocuSign allow researchers and partners to sign contracts remotely, reducing bureaucracy.

Below is an example of how a university might use blockchain to record research findings:

python

```python
import hashlib
import datetime

class ResearchBlockchain:
    def __init__(self):
        self.chain = []
        self.create_block(previous_hash='0', data="Genesis Block")

    def create_block(self, previous_hash, data):
        block = {
            'index': len(self.chain) + 1,
            'timestamp': str(datetime.datetime.now()),
            'date': date,
            'previous_hash': previous_hash,
            'hash': self.hash_block(data, previous_hash)
        }
        self.chain.append(block)
        return block

    @staticmethod
    def hash_block(data, previous_hash):
        to_hash = data + previous_hash + str(datetime.datetime.now())
        return hashlib.sha256(to_hash.encode()).hexdigest()

    def display_chain(self):
        for block in self.chain:
            print(block)

# Registering a research discovery
blockchain = ResearchBlockchain()
blockchain.create_block(previous_hash=blockchain.chain[-1]
```

```
['hash'], data="Discovery of new material for solar cells")
blockchain.create_block(previous_hash=blockchain.chain[-1]
['hash'], data="Method for improving battery efficiency")
blockchain.display_chain()
```

This script can be integrated into IP management systems to record academic innovations and track their use.

IP in education and research is fundamental to protecting knowledge, encouraging innovation and promoting economic and social development. With effective strategies, digital tools and strong collaborations, universities and researchers can maximize the impact of their discoveries while ensuring fair benefits for all parties involved. Technology transfer, in particular, demonstrates how academia can become an engine of transformation for society.

CHAPTER 20: GLOBAL ECONOMIC IMPACTS OF IP

Intellectual property (IP) plays a vital role in global economic development, being one of the main drivers of innovation, competitiveness and growth in various sectors. IP directly influences the way companies create, protect and market products and services, while driving the creation of jobs, increased productivity and the attraction of foreign investment. This chapter explores the economic contribution of IP, highlighting the most influenced sectors and the data that illustrates its impact on a global scale.

Contribution of IP to the Global Economy

IP is closely linked to innovation, which is one of the primary factors of sustainable economic growth. IP rights, such as patents, trademarks and copyrights, provide economic incentives for companies and individuals to invest time and resources in developing new products and technologies. Below are some of the main economic impacts of IP:

1. Stimulating Innovation

The protection offered by IP rights encourages companies and individuals to innovate, guaranteeing exclusivity for a specified period. This exclusivity allows innovators to recoup significant investments in research and development (R&D), fostering a continuous cycle of innovation.

2. Job Generation

IP-intensive sectors such as technology, pharmaceuticals and entertainment are responsible for millions of jobs around the world. Jobs in these sectors generally offer higher than average wages, contributing to increased income and economic well-being.

3. International Trade

IP plays a critical role in international trade. Products and services protected by IP rights, such as luxury brands, software and films, are highly valued in global markets. Exports of IP-intensive goods generate significant revenues for many countries, especially developed economies.

4. Attracting Foreign Investment

Multinational companies often consider a country's IP environment before investing. Countries with robust and well-implemented IP systems attract more foreign investment, as they offer a safe environment for product innovation and commercialization.

Data on the Economic Impact of IP

Studies carried out by international organizations, such as the World Intellectual Property Organization (WIPO) and the Organization for Economic Co-operation and Development (OECD), reveal impressive data on the economic impact of IP:

- **Contribution to GDP**: In advanced economies such as the United States and the European Union, IP-intensive sectors contribute more than 40% of Gross Domestic Product (GDP).
- **Jobs Created**: IP-related sectors employ around 30% of the workforce in many developed countries.
- **Export Revenue**: IP-protected products represent more than 50% of global exports of manufactured goods.

Sectors Most Influenced by IP

Although IP affects almost every sector of the economy, some are particularly dependent on it to prosper. These sectors include technology, pharmaceuticals, entertainment, fashion and manufacturing.

1. Technology

The technology sector is perhaps the most dependent on IP. Patents are fundamental to protecting innovations in hardware, software, artificial intelligence and communications. Companies like Apple, Google and Microsoft invest billions of dollars annually in R&D, knowing that their innovations will be protected.

2. Pharmaceuticals

IP is critical in the pharmaceutical sector, where the development of new medicines requires massive investments in research. Patents allow pharmaceutical companies to recover these costs and fund future discoveries.

3. Entertainment

Copyright underpins the entertainment industry, protecting films, music, video games and other creative content. These rights allow artists and companies to generate substantial income while promoting cultural diversity.

4. Fashion

In the fashion sector, trademarks and industrial designs protect brand identity and help differentiate products. IP protection allows fashion companies to profit from their exclusive creations.

5. Manufacturing

Patents play an essential role in manufacturing, protecting innovative processes and products. This includes everything from new materials to automated production technologies.

Technological Solutions to Assess and Monitor the Economic Impact of IP

Technological tools are increasingly used to assess and monitor the economic impact of IP. These tools include big data, artificial intelligence and blockchain.

Below is an example of Python code that can be used to analyze PI data and generate insights into economic trends:

python

```python
import pandas as pd
import matplotlib.pyplot as plt

def analyze_patent_data(file_path):
    """
    Analyze patent data to identify trends and economic impacts.
    :param file_path: str - Path to the CSV file containing patent
data
    """
    try:
        data = pd.read_csv(file_path)
        yearly_data = data.groupby('Year')['Patents Granted'].sum()

        plt.figure(figsize=(10, 6))
        plt.plot(yearly_data.index, yearly_data.values, marker='o')
        plt.title("Yearly Patents Granted and Economic Trends")
        plt.xlabel("Year")
        plt.ylabel("Number of Patents Granted")
        plt.grid()
        plt.show()
    except Exception as e:
        print(f"Error: {e}")

file_path = "patent_data.csv"
analyze_patent_data(file_path)
```

This script analyzes patent grant data over time, allowing you to identify economic trends related to IP.

Challenges and Opportunities

Despite its importance, the IP system faces significant challenges, such as piracy, counterfeiting and inequalities in access to protected technologies. However, there are also opportunities to improve the economic impact of IP:

1. **Strengthening IP Systems**: Countries can modernize their IP legislation to better protect the rights of innovators.
2. **Education and Training**: Educational programs can help companies and individuals understand the importance of IP and how to use it strategically.
3. **International Collaboration**: Harmonizing global IP standards can facilitate cross-border trade and innovation.

IP is an essential pillar of the global economy, underpinning innovation, trade and job creation. As the world continues to evolve, the importance of IP will only increase, requiring robust strategies to maximize its economic benefits while facing the challenges of an ever-changing global marketplace. Collaboration between governments, businesses and international organizations will be crucial to ensure the IP system continues to promote sustainable growth across sectors.

CHAPTER 21: FUTURE LEGAL CHALLENGES

Digital transformation is redefining every aspect of society, including the way intellectual property (IP) is created, used and protected. The convergence of emerging technologies such as artificial intelligence (AI), blockchain, Internet of Things (IoT) and big data brings a number of legal challenges that require urgent attention to ensure that legal systems are able to keep up with rapid technological evolution. This chapter addresses the main impacts of digital transformation on IP legislation, identifies legal gaps and suggests possible adaptations to face these challenges.

Impacts of Digital Transformation on IP Legislation

The digital era has brought profound changes to the creation, sharing and commercialization of intangible assets. Although IP was designed to protect intellectual creations, technological advances are testing the limits of existing legal frameworks.

1. Artificial Intelligence and Authorship

Artificial intelligence is becoming a driving force of innovation, generating works ranging from music and visual art to software code and scientific inventions. The fundamental question is: who should be considered the author or inventor in AI-generated works? Current legislation often requires human authorship to grant IP rights, creating a significant gap in the protection of machine-generated creations.

2. Blockchain and Proof of Ownership

Blockchain is being widely adopted as a solution for tracking and authenticating intellectual property. The decentralized and immutable nature of blockchain offers a robust alternative to traditional IP registration systems. However, current legal systems still do not widely recognize blockchain-based records as proof of ownership, creating barriers to their widespread adoption.

3. Internet of Things and Patents

The Internet of Things connects devices in unprecedented ways, creating an ecosystem of interdependent technologies. This environment increases the complexity of protecting technological innovations, as it often involves multiple patent holders and systems operating together. Gaps in IP legislation can make it difficult to resolve disputes and commercialize IoT-based technologies.

4. Big Data and Copyright

Big data depends on the collection, processing and analysis of large volumes of data. The ownership and use of this data are often not clearly defined in current legislation. Furthermore, the use of copyrighted data to train AI algorithms raises questions about IP infringement and the right to consent.

Legal Gaps

Legal gaps in IP legislation represent a significant challenge for governments, companies and creators. Some of these gaps include:

- **Lack of clarity on AI authorship**: Many countries have not yet defined how to treat machine-generated creations in their IP legislation.
- **Incompatibility with emerging technologies**: Traditional legal frameworks were not designed to handle the decentralization and automation introduced by technologies like blockchain and IoT.
- **Inadequate data protection**: The absence of clear regulations on data ownership creates uncertainty that can harm innovation and business.
- **Gaps in global protection**: Differences between IP

legislation in different countries make it difficult to protect assets on a global scale.

Possible Adaptations to Face Challenges

To deal with the challenges presented by digital transformation, legal systems need to evolve. Some possible adaptations include:

1. Update Authorship Requirements

IP legislations should consider the inclusion of AI-generated creations, allowing human authors or companies using AI to claim rights to these works. Alternatively, a new category of rights specific to AI creations could be created, ensuring that these works are adequately protected.

2. Legal Recognition of Blockchain

Legal systems must recognize blockchain-based IP records as proof of ownership. This would require the standardization of blockchain systems to ensure their reliability and interoperability.

3. Patent Reforms for IoT

Reforms to patent laws can help address the complexities of IoT, including creating mechanisms to resolve disputes involving multiple patent holders and streamlining licensing processes.

4. Data Regulation

Data protection must be expanded to include clear guidelines on the ownership, use and sharing of data in commercial and research contexts. This may include establishing specific rules for the use of IP-protected data in training AI algorithms.

Technological Tools to Address Legal Challenges

Digital technologies can also be used to address IP-related legal challenges. Below are some practical applications:

IP Registration System with Blockchain

Blockchain can be used to create a decentralized IP registration system, ensuring that information about intellectual property is stored securely and accessible. The code below demonstrates how to register a patent on a blockchain system:

python

```python
import hashlib
import datetime

class Blockchain:
    def __init__(self):
        self.chain = []
        self.create_block(previous_hash='0', data="Genesis Block")

    def create_block(self, previous_hash, data):
        block = {
            'index': len(self.chain) + 1,
            'timestamp': str(datetime.datetime.now()),
            'date': date,
            'previous_hash': previous_hash,
            'hash': self.hash_block(data, previous_hash)
        }
        self.chain.append(block)
        return block

    @staticmethod
    def hash_block(data, previous_hash):
        to_hash = data + previous_hash + str(datetime.datetime.now())
        return hashlib.sha256(to_hash.encode()).hexdigest()

    def display_chain(self):
        for block in self.chain:
            print(block)

# Registering a patent
blockchain = Blockchain()
blockchain.create_block(previous_hash=blockchain.chain[-1]['hash'], data="Patent: AI-driven medical diagnosis system")
```

```
blockchain.display_chain()
```

This system records patent information on a blockchain, creating an immutable record that can be used to prove intellectual property.

IP Misuse Monitoring with AI

AI-based systems can track PI misuse in real time by analyzing large volumes of online data. This could include tracking unauthorized copies of copyrighted content or monitoring trademark infringements on digital marketplaces.

Automation of Licensing Agreements

Smart contract technology can be used to automate the IP licensing process, ensuring that contract terms are applied transparently and efficiently.

Future legal challenges related to IP require a proactive and collaborative approach between governments, companies and technology experts. Adapting legislation to deal with the complexities of digital transformation is essential to protect innovation, promote economic growth and ensure fairness in the use and sharing of intellectual property. By combining legal reforms with innovative technological solutions, it will be possible to address these challenges and build an IP system that meets the demands of a rapidly evolving world.

CHAPTER 22: IP IN THE PUBLIC SECTOR

Intellectual property (IP) in the public sector plays a crucial role in promoting innovation, economic development and providing effective services to society. Governments and public organizations are not only users of IP, but also significant creators of intellectual assets. Strategic protection and use of these assets can lead to improvements in public services, revenue generation, and stimulation of research and development.

Protection and Use of IP in Governments and Public Organizations

Governments and public organizations produce a wide range of IP assets, including software, databases, publications, patents resulting from government research, trademarks and designs. Protecting these assets is essential to ensure they can be used in a way that maximizes public benefit while preventing unauthorized or harmful uses.

1. Government Patents

Government agencies often conduct research that results in patentable innovations. Institutions such as national laboratories, public universities and research centers develop technologies that can be applied in various sectors, from health to defense. Patent protection allows the government to control the use of these innovations, being able to license them to the private sector or use them for public purposes.

2. Software and Databases

Governments develop software and databases to manage information, provide services to citizens and support decision-making. Protecting these assets under appropriate copyrights and licenses is crucial to maintaining information integrity and security. Additionally, decisions about whether software should be open source or proprietary affect collaboration with the private sector and other institutions.

3. Brands and Visual Identity

Public organizations use brands and visual identities to distinguish their services and promote government initiatives. Protecting these marks prevents confusion and misuse that could harm the government's reputation or mislead the public.

4. PI Sharing Policies

Governments can choose to share their IP assets to encourage innovation and economic development. This can be done through open licensing, granting rights to companies or public-private partnerships. Such policies must balance the need to protect public interests with stimulating economic activity.

5. Protection of State Secrets

Some government information, especially related to national security and defense, is protected as state secrets. Proper management of this sensitive information is critical to national security and requires rigorous policies and procedures.

Global Examples

USA

In the United States, the federal government is one of the largest patent holders. The Bayh-Dole Act allows institutions that receive federal research funding, such as universities and small businesses, to retain IP rights resulting from their discoveries. This encouraged the commercialization of technologies and strengthened technology transfer between the public and private sector.

Agencies like NASA and the Department of Energy have robust technology licensing programs. NASA, for example, makes patents available for commercial licensing, allowing private companies to use technologies developed for space exploration in terrestrial products and services.

European Union

In the European Union, IP policies aim to harmonize the protection and use of intellectual assets among member states. EU-funded projects such as Horizon Europe encourage innovation and often result in IP assets that must be managed in accordance with EU guidelines.

National governments also implement their own policies. The United Kingdom, for example, through the Intellectual Property Office (IPO), provides guidance to public organizations on how to manage and protect their IP assets, promoting effective use for the benefit of society.

China

China has made significant efforts to strengthen IP protection in the public sector. Government institutions and universities are registering an increasing number of patents, reflecting the national strategy to boost technological innovation. The Chinese government also encourages the transfer of technology from public institutions to the private sector, aiming for economic development.

Brazil

In Brazil, the Technological Innovation Law establishes guidelines to stimulate scientific research, innovation and IP protection in public institutions. The law allows public universities and research institutes to license their innovations to private companies, encouraging collaboration and the development of national technologies.

India

India has implemented policies to promote IP protection in public organizations. The Council of Scientific and Industrial Research

(CSIR) is one of the largest patent holding entities in India, with a diverse portfolio that includes technologies in biotechnology, pharmaceuticals and renewable energy. The government encourages the commercialization of these technologies through licensing and partnerships.

Tools and Strategies for IP Management in the Public Sector

1. Technology Transfer Offices

Many public organizations have established offices dedicated to IP management and technology transfer. These offices are responsible for identifying innovations, protecting intellectual assets, negotiating licensing agreements and promoting partnerships with the private sector.

2. Open Licensing Policies

Governments may choose to license certain IP assets under open terms, allowing third parties to use, modify and distribute the material. This is common in open source software and open data projects, which encourage innovation and transparency.

For example, governments can release public datasets under permissive licenses, allowing companies and developers to create applications and services that benefit society. Below is an example of how an open license might be structured:

text

Open Government Data License:

1. Permission to Use: You are authorized to use, modify and distribute the data provided without restrictions.
2. Attribution: You must give appropriate credit to the government as the source of the data.
3. No Warranty: Data is provided "as is" without warranties of any kind.
4. No Endorsement: Use of data does not imply endorsement by the government.

3. Public-Private Partnerships

Partnerships between governments and the private sector are effective strategies for developing and commercializing technologies. These partnerships allow public organizations to leverage private sector resources and expertise, while private companies gain access to government IP assets and innovations.

4. Use of Digital Technologies for IP Management

Governments are adopting technologies such as IP management systems and digital platforms to improve efficiency in managing intellectual assets. This includes using databases to track patents and copyrights, as well as online platforms to facilitate licensing.

Below is an example of how a Python script can be used to extract patent information from a public database:

python

```python
import requests

def get_patent_info(patent_number):
    """
    Retrieve patent information from a public government
database.
    :param patent_number: str - The patent number to search for
    :return: dict - Patent details
    """
    api_url = f"https://api.patents.gov/getPatent?number={patent_number}"
    try:
        response = requests.get(api_url)
        if response.status_code == 200:
            patent_data = response.json()
            return {
                'title': patent_data['title'],
                'inventors': patent_data['inventors'],
```

```
            'filing_date': patent_data['filingDate'],
            'assignee': patent_data['assignee'],
            'abstract': patent_data['abstract']
        }
    else:
        return {'error': 'Patent not found'}
except Exception as e:
    return {'error': str(e)}

# Example usage
patent_number = 'US1234567A'
patent_info = get_patent_info(patent_number)
print(patent_info)
```

This script demonstrates how to access patent information made available by a government, allowing public organizations to manage and monitor IP assets.

Challenges in IP Management in the Public Sector

1. Limited Resources

Many public organizations face budget constraints that make it difficult to effectively manage IP. This can lead to underutilization of intellectual assets or a lack of adequate protection, exposing the government to potential losses.

2. Legal Complexity

IP laws can be complex and vary between jurisdictions. Governments must navigate these legal systems to protect their assets, which requires specialized expertise.

3. Balance between Transparency and Protection

Governments have a responsibility to be transparent with citizens, but they also need to protect sensitive information and IP assets. Finding the balance between openness and protection is a constant challenge.

4. Security Risks

IP asset management, especially in the digital context, presents security risks. Protection against cyberattacks and information leaks is essential to maintaining the integrity of government assets.

Intellectual property in the public sector is a vital area that requires strategic attention. By protecting and effectively utilizing their IP assets, governments and public organizations can drive innovation, improve public services and contribute to economic development. Clear policies, investments in institutional capacity and collaboration with the private sector are key components for success in this area.

Understanding the challenges and opportunities associated with IP management in the public sector is essential to maximize public benefit and ensure that innovations developed with government resources are used in ways that serve the interests of society as a whole.

CHAPTER 23: TOOLS FOR GLOBAL PI

Globalization and digital transformation require innovative approaches to managing intellectual property (IP) on a global scale. With the increasing interconnectedness of markets and rapid technological evolution, creators and businesses face significant challenges in protecting, monitoring and expanding their IP assets. Fortunately, a wide range of digital tools and resources are available to facilitate these processes. This chapter presents key platforms and resources that help individuals and organizations manage their IP effectively, ensuring protection and maximizing value in global markets.

Digital Platforms for IP Monitoring and Registration

Digital platforms play a crucial role in monitoring and recording IP, allowing users to track violations, register new assets and manage portfolios across multiple jurisdictions.

1. WIPO IP Portal

THE **WIPO IP Portal** is a centralized platform offered by the World Intellectual Property Organization (WIPO) for IP-related services. It gives you access to essential tools, including:

- **PATENTSCOPE**: Allows searches in a global patent database.
- **Madrid Monitor**: Facilitates the monitoring of trademarks registered by the Madrid System.
- **Hague System**: Assists with managing industrial design records.

These tools help users register and monitor IP assets across multiple countries, simplifying the process for creators and businesses operating globally.

2. USPTO e EPO

The United States (USPTO) and European (EPO) patent offices are leaders in providing robust digital resources for IP. Both offer platforms for:

- **Patent Search**: Access to detailed records of granted patents and application publications.
- **Trademark Registrations**: Tools for searching trademarks and tracking orders.
- **Portfolio Management**: Online services to manage existing assets.

Furthermore, these platforms integrate APIs that allow the automation of monitoring and analysis processes.

3. TMview e DesignView

Developed by the European Union Intellectual Property Office (EUIPO), the tools **TMview** and **DesignView** allow global searches of trademark and industrial design registrations, respectively. With the participation of more than 70 national and regional offices, these tools are indispensable for identifying possible conflicts and opportunities for expansion.

4. Blockchain Tools for PI

Blockchain technology is emerging as a powerful solution for recording and managing IP. Platforms like **IBM IPwe** and **KODAK One** offer blockchain-based solutions for:

- Registration of intellectual assets with immutable date and time.
- Management of licenses and royalties automated by smart contracts.
- Content traceability and authentication.

Below is an example script that demonstrates how to use blockchain to record basic PI information:

python

```
import hashlib
```

```
import datetime

class Blockchain:
    def __init__(self):
        self.chain = []
        self.create_block(previous_hash='0', data="Genesis Block")

    def create_block(self, previous_hash, data):
        block = {
            'index': len(self.chain) + 1,
            'timestamp': str(datetime.datetime.now()),
            'date': date,
            'previous_hash': previous_hash,
            'hash': self.hash_block(data, previous_hash)
        }
        self.chain.append(block)
        return block

    @staticmethod
    def hash_block(data, previous_hash):
        to_hash = data + previous_hash +
str(datetime.datetime.now())
        return hashlib.sha256(to_hash.encode()).hexdigest()

    def display_chain(self):
        for block in self.chain:
            print(block)

# Registering a trademark
blockchain = Blockchain()
blockchain.create_block(previous_hash=blockchain.chain[-1]
['hash'], data="Trademark: UniqueApp Logo")
blockchain.display_chain()
```

This example records IP assets on a blockchain, creating reliable and accessible records.

Useful Resources for Creators and Businesses

In addition to digital platforms, creators and businesses can benefit from a range of additional features that help with IP management in global markets.

1. Breach Monitoring Tools

Continuous monitoring is essential to identify and take action against potential IP violations. Tools like **BrandShield** and **MarkMonitor** are designed to track trademark, copyright, and design violations across digital and physical platforms.

A practical example is the use of automated scripts to monitor possible misuse of trademarks on marketplaces:

python

```python
import requests
from bs4 import BeautifulSoup

def monitor_marketplace(brand_name, marketplace_url):
    """
    Monitor a marketplace for potential trademark infringement.
    :param brand_name: str - The brand name to search for
    :param marketplace_url: str - URL of the marketplace
    :return: list - List of product listings mentioning the brand name
    """
    try:
        response = requests.get(marketplace_url)
        if response.status_code == 200:
            soup = BeautifulSoup(response.content, "html.parser")
            listings = soup.find_all("div", class_="product-title") # Adjust based on marketplace structure
            infringements = [listing.text for listing in listings if brand_name.lower() in listing.text.lower()]
            return infringements
        else:
```

```
        return []
    except Exception as e:
        return f"Error: {str(e)}"

marketplace = "https://examplemarketplace.com"
brand = "ProtectedBrand"

infringing_listings = monitor_marketplace(brand, marketplace)
if infringing_listings:
    print("Potential infringements found:")
    for listing in infringing_listings:
        print(listing)
else:
    print("No infringements detected.")
```

This approach can be expanded to monitor multiple marketplaces or social media platforms.

2. Education and Training

Organizations like WIPO Academy offer online courses and IP training programs, covering topics such as patents, copyright, trademarks and asset management. These resources are valuable for creators and companies who want to better understand how to protect and commercialize their IP.

3. Collaboration Networks

Platforms like **InnoCentive** and **NineSigma** connect companies with global innovators, promoting collaboration on R&D projects. These networks can be an opportunity to license IP or seek solutions to technical challenges.

4. Portfolio Management Tools

Systems like **Anaqua** and **CPA Global** enable companies to centrally manage their IP portfolios, tracking assets, renewal deadlines and licenses. These systems offer detailed analyzes that help in making strategic decisions.

5. PI Data and Reports

Access to up-to-date data is essential for strategic decisions. Databases like **World Intellectual Property Indicators** and **Statesman** provide insights into global IP trends, helping companies identify opportunities and assess risks.

Strategies for Optimizing the Use of Digital Tools

To make the most of the digital tools available, creators and companies must adopt well-defined strategies:

- **Choosing the Right Tool**: Assess the organization's specific needs before investing in IP platforms or services.
- **Process Automation**: Use custom APIs and scripts to integrate tools and automate repetitive tasks.
- **Continuous Monitoring**: Establish systems to monitor IP violations in real time, enabling rapid responses.
- **Collaboration with Experts**: Work with lawyers and IP consultants to ensure assets are managed effectively.

The digital tools and resources described in this chapter are fundamental to managing IP in a global environment. As markets continue to interconnect and technologies evolve, strategic use of these tools will be increasingly important for creators and companies looking to protect and maximize the value of their intellectual assets. By combining technology, knowledge and a proactive approach, it is possible to face challenges and seize opportunities in the global IP scenario.

CHAPTER 24: ETHICS AND INTELLECTUAL PROPERTY

Ethics in intellectual property (IP) is a central topic in discussions that seek to balance the rights of innovators with fair access to knowledge and technology. IP was designed to encourage innovation by granting temporary exclusivity to creators. However, its use and implementation often raise ethical questions, especially when public needs conflict with private rights. This chapter explores ethical reflections on IP, analyzing contemporary challenges and proposing ways to balance innovation and access.

Reflections on the Balance between Innovation and Access

The PI system is, by design, a delicate balance. On the one hand, it protects the rights of creators and companies by offering financial incentives to invest in research and development. On the other hand, he must ensure that the public benefits from innovations, especially in critical areas such as health, education and the environment.

1. Patents and Access to Medicines

One of the most discussed ethical dilemmas in IP is related to pharmaceutical patents. The exclusivity granted by patents allows companies to recover the high costs of research and development, but can also result in high prices for essential medicines, making them unaffordable for vulnerable populations.

Cases such as the HIV/AIDS pandemic in sub-Saharan Africa illustrate this dilemma. Antiretroviral drugs were initially inaccessible to millions due to the high cost of patents. Pressure from non-governmental organizations and compulsory licensing initiatives have helped drive down prices, raising questions about how to balance corporate interests with public health needs.

2. Copyright and Education

Copyright plays a crucial role in protecting literary, scientific and artistic works. However, strict enforcement of these rights can hinder access to knowledge, especially in low- and middle-income countries. Educational resources such as textbooks and scientific publications are often inaccessible due to financial barriers, limiting educational and scientific development.

The growing adoption of open access licenses, such as those offered by Creative Commons, demonstrates an attempt to address this issue by allowing authors to share their works with minimal restrictions, promoting access to knowledge while maintaining control over their rights.

3. Artificial Intelligence and Authorship Ethics

With the rise of artificial intelligence (AI), new ethical questions emerge. AI systems can create works of art, music, texts and even technical inventions. Recognition of authorship and the rights associated with these creations raise questions about how the IP system should evolve to address non-human creations.

For example, if an AI algorithm generates a new musical composition, who should receive the copyright? The programmer, the owner of the AI system, or the AI as an independent entity? These issues require deep ethical reflections and adjustments to IP legislation.

4. Biopiracy and Traditional Knowledge

Biopiracy, or the misappropriation of genetic resources and traditional knowledge, is a significant ethical issue. Indigenous and local communities often do not receive recognition or compensation for the commercial use of their knowledge. This creates an imbalance of power and justice, reinforcing the need for systems that protect these rights.

Instruments such as the Nagoya Protocol attempt to address these concerns by requiring prior consent and benefit sharing when accessing genetic resources and associated knowledge. However, effective implementation of these guidelines still faces challenges.

Contemporary Ethical Challenges

As technologies evolve, ethical challenges in IP become more complex, requiring dynamic and innovative responses.

1. Innovation Monopolies

IP can inadvertently create monopolies that limit competition and access. Large companies often accumulate extensive patent portfolios, creating barriers to entry for startups and small businesses. This behavior, known as "patent trolling," raises ethical concerns about using IP to block innovation rather than promote it.

2. Effects of Globalization

Globalization has increased the need for harmonization of IP laws, but it has also highlighted inequalities between developed and developing countries. While the former often hold the majority of IP assets, the latter often depend on access to protected technologies, creating tensions over how to balance global rights and local needs.

3. Use of Personal Data and Intellectual Property

With the growth of big data and AI, the collection and use of personal data raises ethical questions about privacy and ownership. Data used to train algorithms is often collected without individuals' explicit consent, creating a dilemma about the ethical boundaries between technological innovation and respect for privacy.

4. Sustainability and Intellectual Property

Sustainable development depends on innovations in renewable energy, agriculture and green technologies. Strict IP protection can hinder the dissemination of these technologies in countries that need them most, raising questions about how the IP system can be adapted to promote global sustainability.

Paths to Ethical Resolution

Responding to the ethical challenges of IP requires a multifaceted approach that combines legal reforms, voluntary initiatives and technological advances.

1. Reforms to IP Laws

Governments and international organizations must work to reform IP laws, ensuring they are more inclusive and adapted to contemporary needs. This includes:

- Introduction of mechanisms that encourage voluntary licensing and technology transfer.
- Review of patentability requirements to prevent abuse and monopolies.
- Recognition of traditional knowledge and protection of indigenous communities.

2. Open Access Promotion

Open access models, such as Creative Commons licenses and initiatives like the Open Access Movement, can help democratize knowledge and promote global collaboration. Universities and governments can play a leading role by adopting and promoting open access policies.

3. Technological Tools for IP Ethics

Technology can be an ally in resolving IP ethical issues. Blockchain-based tools can create transparent records of intellectual property, ensuring traceability and fair recognition. Below is an example of how blockchain can be applied to monitor the ethical use of IP assets:

python

```
import hashlib
```

```python
import datetime

class EthicalIPBlockchain:
    def __init__(self):
        self.chain = []
        self.create_block(previous_hash='0', data="Genesis Block")

    def create_block(self, previous_hash, data):
        block = {
            'index': len(self.chain) + 1,
            'timestamp': str(datetime.datetime.now()),
            'date': date,
            'previous_hash': previous_hash,
            'hash': self.hash_block(data, previous_hash)
        }
        self.chain.append(block)
        return block

    @staticmethod
    def hash_block(data, previous_hash):
        to_hash = data + previous_hash + str(datetime.datetime.now())
        return hashlib.sha256(to_hash.encode()).hexdigest()

    def display_chain(self):
        for block in self.chain:
            print(block)

# Tracking ethical use of IP
blockchain = EthicalIPBlockchain()
blockchain.create_block(previous_hash=blockchain.chain[-1]
['hash'], data="License granted for green technology to developing
nation")
blockchain.create_block(previous_hash=blockchain.chain[-1]
['hash'], data="Knowledge shared under fair terms with
indigenous community")
blockchain.display_chain()
```

This application can be used to monitor ethical commitments related to IP, increasing transparency and accountability.

4. Education and Awareness

Educating creators, companies and the public about the ethical aspects of IP is critical. Training programs and awareness campaigns can help build a culture of accountability and collaboration.

IP ethics is an essential issue in a constantly evolving world. Balancing innovation and access requires creative, collaborative solutions that respect creators' rights while meeting society's needs. By addressing contemporary ethical challenges seriously, the IP system can become a powerful force for human progress, ensuring that innovation benefits everyone in an equitable and sustainable way.

CHAPTER 25: IP PRACTICAL GUIDE

Managing and protecting intellectual property (IP) effectively is essential for creators, entrepreneurs and businesses. This practical guide provides checklists, contract templates and detailed steps for IP registration, with guidance that can be adapted for different international legislation. The hands-on approach ensures users can navigate the complex PI system with clarity and confidence.

Checklists for IP Management

Checklists are valuable tools for organizing and ensuring that no important details are overlooked in the IP protection and management process.

1. Checklist for Patent Registration

- **Innovation Assessment**
  - Is the invention new and non-obvious?
  - Does the innovation have industrial application?
- **Required Documentation**
  - Detailed description of the invention.
  - Technical drawings or diagrams.
  - Test or study reports.
- **Choice of Jurisdiction**
  - National, regional (EPO, ARIPO) or international (PCT) registration?
- **Submission Protocol**
  - Filling out the order form.
  - Payment of registration fees.
  - Submission of documents to the competent office.

2. Checklist for Trademark Registration

- **Availability Search**
  - Is the trademark already registered in another jurisdiction?
  - Does the name or logo violate third-party rights?
- **Required Documentation**
  - Logo or visual design.
  - Declaration of use or intention to use.
- **Choosing Registration Class**
  - Identification of appropriate classes in the Nice Classification System.
- **Submission**
  - Completing the registration form.
  - Payment of applicable fees.

3. Copyright Checklist

- **Identification of the Work**
  - Is the work original and can it be protected?
  - Is it a literary, musical, artistic work or software?
- **Documentation**
  - Copy of the work in physical or digital format.
  - Declaration of authorship.
- **Record**
  - Submission to the copyright office or equivalent institution.

Contract Templates

Contract templates are essential for formalizing IP-related agreements, such as licensing, assignment of rights and collaboration.

1. Licensing Agreement Template

text

Licensing Agreement

This Licensing Agreement ("Agreement") is made and entered into as of [Date], by and between:

Licensor: [Name and Address]
Licensee: [Name and Address]

1. Grant of License:
The Licensor grants the Licensee a [exclusive/non-exclusive] license to use the intellectual property described as [Description of Intellectual Property].

2. Term and Termination:
This Agreement shall remain in effect for [Duration], unless terminated earlier by either party with [Notice Period] notice.

3. Royalties:
The Licensee agrees to pay a royalty of [Percentage or Fixed Amount] on [Sales/Revenue] generated using the licensed property.

4. Confidentiality:
Both parties agree to maintain the confidentiality of proprietary information related to this Agreement.

5. Governing Law:
This Agreement shall be governed by the laws of [Jurisdiction].

Signed,
[Licensor Signature]   [Licensee Signature]

2. Assignment of Rights Agreement Model
text

Assignment of Intellectual Property Rights

This Assignment Agreement ("Agreement") is made and entered into as of [Date], by and between:
Assignor: [Name and Address]
Assignee: [Name and Address]

1. Assignment:

The Assignor hereby transfers all rights, title, and interest in the intellectual property described as [Description of Intellectual Property] to the Assignee.

2. Consideration:
The Assignee agrees to pay the Assignor [Amount] as consideration for the transfer of rights.

3. Representations and Warranties:
The Assignor represents that they are the sole owner of the intellectual property and have the right to transfer it.

4. Governing Law:
This Agreement shall be governed by the laws of [Jurisdiction].

Signed,
[Assignor Signature]   [Assignee Signature]

3. Non-Disclosure Agreement (NDA) Template
text

Non-Disclosure Agreement (NDA)

This Non-Disclosure Agreement ("Agreement") is made and entered into as of [Date], by and between:
Disclosing Party: [Name and Address]
Receiving Party: [Name and Address]

1. Confidential Information:
Confidential Information includes [Description of Information], whether disclosed in written, oral, or electronic form.

2. Obligations:
The Receiving Party agrees to maintain the confidentiality of the disclosed information and not to disclose it to third parties.

3. Term:

The obligations under this Agreement shall remain in effect for [Duration] after termination.

4. Governing Law:

This Agreement shall be governed by the laws of [Jurisdiction].

Signed,

[Disclosing Party Signature]   [Receiving Party Signature]

Steps for IP Registration

1. Patents

1. Carry out a prior search to ensure the novelty of the invention.
2. Prepare detailed technical documentation.
3. Choose the appropriate jurisdiction for registration.
4. Submit the request to the appropriate office and pay the fees.
5. Monitor the examination process and respond to additional requests.

2. Brands

1. Conduct a trademark search to avoid conflicts.
2. Choose relevant classes based on intended use.
3. Submit the application and pay the fees.
4. Monitor the publication for objections by third parties.
5. Obtain the registration certificate.

3. Copyright

1. Identify the type of work and appropriate jurisdiction.
2. Gather the necessary documentation to prove authorship.
3. Register the work with the official body.
4. Receive the registration certificate.

Adaptation to Different Legislations

The IP system varies significantly between countries, requiring creators and companies to adapt their strategies based on jurisdiction. Some considerations include:

- **USA**: The first-to-file system applies to patents, highlighting the importance of registering innovations quickly.
- **European Union**: IP registration is harmonized in several areas, such as trademarks and industrial designs, allowing protection in all Member States.
- **China**: Strengthening local protection with IP registrations is essential due to the large domestic market and compliance challenges.
- **Brazil**: The National Institute of Industrial Property (INPI) regulates patents, trademarks and other IP rights, but the process can take longer due to high volumes of applications.

Use of Digital Tools

Digital tools can make IP management easier. Below is an example script for monitoring PI renewal deadlines:

python

```python
import datetime

def monitor_renewal(deadlines):
    """
    Monitor renewal deadlines for intellectual property assets.
    :param deadlines: dict - Dictionary of asset names and renewal dates
    :return: list - List of assets nearing renewal
    """
    today = datetime.date.today()
    nearing_renewal = []

    for asset, deadline in deadlines.items():
        days_left = (deadline - today).days
        if days_left <= 30:
```

```
        nearing_renewal.append((asset, days_left))

    return nearing_renewal

# Example usage
renewal_deadlines = {
    "Trademark A": datetime.date(2024, 5, 15),
    "Patent B": datetime.date(2024, 6, 1),
    "Copyright C": datetime.date(2024, 4, 20),
}

upcoming_renewals = monitor_renewal(renewal_deadlines)
for asset, days in upcoming_renewals:
    print(f"Asset '{asset}' is due for renewal in {days} days.")
```

This script helps you track critical deadlines, ensuring that IP assets are not lost due to late renewals.

This practical guide offers a clear and adaptable framework for protecting and managing IP. From detailed checklists to contract templates and technology tools, the resources provided help creators and businesses navigate the challenges of the IP system in different jurisdictions. With well-defined strategies, it is possible to maximize the value of intellectual assets and ensure that they are protected in a competitive global scenario.

FINAL CONCLUSION

The conclusion of this book offers a comprehensive overview of the themes explored throughout our 25 chapters, highlighting the essential learnings from each section. Intellectual property (IP) was unveiled in its multiple dimensions, from fundamental concepts to ethical challenges and practical solutions, providing a journey rich in knowledge.

Chapter 1: Introduction to Intellectual Property
In this chapter, we establish the foundations of the IP concept, addressing its definition, economic importance and cultural impact. We explore how IP fosters innovation and protects the rights of creators, while stimulating social and economic development.

Chapter 2: History and Evolution of IP
We present the historical trajectory of IP, from the first patent laws to global agreements such as TRIPS. The evolution of standards reflects the need to balance local and global interests, shaping IP as a pillar of international trade and innovation.

Chapter 3: Copyright
We discuss the protection of literary, artistic and scientific works, explaining the global structure of copyright and the challenges faced in a digitalized world. Issues such as licensing and digital piracy were addressed with practical examples.

Chapter 4: Brands and Business Identity
This chapter explored how brands are fundamental to differentiating products and services in the market. With an emphasis on the Madrid Protocol, we discuss international registration and the strategic value of brands in global commerce.

Chapter 5: Patents

We cover the patent registration process, highlighting differences between jurisdictions such as the US, EU, Japan and China. We analyze how patents promote innovation while creating accessibility challenges in sectors such as pharmaceuticals and technology.

Chapter 6: Industrial Design
We study the protection of industrial designs and their practical application. Global cases have illustrated how design impacts product competitiveness and brand perception.

Chapter 7: Trade Secrets
We analyze the protection of trade secrets as business strategies and formulas. We discuss global regulations and tools for protecting confidential information in a competitive business environment.

Chapter 8: Licensing and International Contracts
Focusing on multilingual contracts, this chapter detailed strategies for licensing and negotiating IP, with examples of best practices for maximizing the economic value of intellectual assets.

Chapter 9: IP in Electronic Commerce
We explore challenges and solutions for protecting digital assets on global marketplaces. Strategies against digital piracy and the importance of monitoring misuse were emphasized.

Chapter 10: Infringements and International Disputes
This chapter analyzed global litigation cases and alternative dispute resolution methods. Reflections on the harmonization of legal standards highlighted the importance of international collaboration.

Chapter 11: Technology Transfer
We discuss how international policies impact developing economies, encouraging innovation and facilitating collaboration between nations.

Chapter 12: Artificial Intelligence and IP

We address debates about authorship of AI-generated works and the associated legal challenges. This chapter brought a futuristic view of IP in a technologically advanced world.

Chapter 13: Strategic IP Management
We determine how to value and manage IP assets in global contexts, presenting practical tools for multinationals and startups.

Chapter 14: IP in the Creative Industry
We explore the impacts of IP in sectors such as fashion, audiovisual, music and games, illustrating examples of success in protecting artistic creations.

Chapter 15: IP and Health
We analyze pharmaceutical patents and ethical debates about global access to essential medicines. Strategies for balancing innovation and social justice were detailed.

Chapter 16: Intellectual Property and Sustainability
This chapter focused on green innovations and how IP can encourage sustainable technologies, promoting environmentally responsible practices.

Chapter 17: IP and Traditional Knowledge
We reflect on the protection of indigenous knowledge and the fight against biopiracy. International conventions such as the Nagoya Protocol were presented as important solutions.

Chapter 18: IP in Startups
We discuss strategies for startups to protect their IP and scale their business. Practical examples and tips for licensing and monetization enriched the content.

Chapter 19: IP in Education and Research
We explore rights to academic publications and technology transfer in universities, focusing on practices that encourage scientific innovation.

Chapter 20: Global Economic Impacts of IP

We analyze data on IP's contribution to the global economy, highlighting most influenced sectors and the economic opportunities created by intellectual assets.

Chapter 21: Future Legal Challenges
We present the impacts of digital transformation on IP legislation and legal gaps to be addressed, with solutions adapted to emerging technologies.

Chapter 22: IP in the Public Sector
We study how governments and public organizations manage and use IP to promote innovation, improve services and protect sensitive information.

Chapter 23: Tools for Global PI
We offer practical insight into digital platforms for monitoring and recording IP, as well as helpful resources for creators and businesses.

Chapter 24: Ethics and Intellectual Property
We reflect on the balance between innovation and access, addressing ethical challenges such as biopiracy, AI and sustainability, with practical and reflective solutions.

Chapter 25: IP Practical Guide
We finish with checklists, contract models and steps for IP registration. This chapter is designed as a practical resource for users in different jurisdictions.

Reflection on the Global and Local Relevance of IP

Intellectual property transcends borders, playing a vital role in economic, cultural and social development. Globally, it promotes innovation and facilitates international trade, while locally, it strengthens national economies, protects cultural traditions and encourages entrepreneurship.

IP is a strategic resource that drives solutions to global challenges, from healthcare to sustainability. However, it requires a balance between exclusive rights and fair access, a goal that can only be achieved through international collaborations and continuous adaptations to technological changes.

I thank you, reader, who went through this learning journey with us, my most sincere thanks. This book was created with the aim of not only informing, but also inspiring the exploration and responsible use of intellectual property as a tool for transformation and progress.

Cordially,
Diego Rodrigues and Team!